Stand Out 5
Grammar Challenge
Second Edition

HEINLE
CENGAGE Learning™

Australia • Brazil • Japan • Korea • Mexico • Singapore • Spain • United Kingdom • United States

Stand Out 5 Grammar Challenge
Staci Johnson and Rob Jenkins

Publisher: Sherrise Roehr

Acquisitions Editor: Tom Jefferies

Director of Content and Media Production:
Michael Burggren

Development Editor: Michael Ryall

Product Marketing Manager: Katie Kelley

Sr. Content Project Editor: Maryellen E. Killeen

Sr. Print Buyer: Mary Beth Hennebury

Development Editor: Carol Crowell

Project Manager: Tunde A. Dewey

Cover / Text Designer: Studio Montage

Compositor: Parkwood Composition
Service, Inc.

ISBN 10: 1-4240-1784-X
ISBN 13: 978-1-4240-1784-3

Heinle
25 Thomson Place
Boston, MA 02210
USA

Cengage Learning is a leading provider of customized learning solutions with office locations around the globe, including Singapore, the United Kingdom, Australia, Mexico, Brazil and Japan. Locate our local office at:
international.cengage.com/region

Cengage Learning products are represented in Canada
by Nelson Education, Ltd.

Visit Heinle online at **elt.heinle.com**
Visit our corporate website at **cengage.com**

Printed in U.S.A.
4 5 6 7 8 9 10 11

CONTENTS

TO THE TEACHER

Stand Out 5 Grammar Challenge challenges students to develop and expand their grammar skills through fifty-nine guided exercises or "challenges."

Each Challenge includes:

▶ **Charts** Clear grammar charts help the teacher lay out the components of structures and provide useful example sentences.

▶ **Notes** Notes within the charts help students understand important shifts in language use and meaning through concise explanations.

▶ **Practice** Exercises challenge students to master grammar structures while reviewing the vocabulary and thematic contexts actively taught in *Stand Out 5 Student Book*. Additional exercises reinforce grammar structures passively introduced in *Stand Out 5 Student Book* contexts.

How to use the *Stand Out 5 Grammar Challenge* workbook

The *Stand Out 5 Grammar Challenge* workbook can be used in a variety of ways:

- The grammar challenges can be assigned daily or on an as-needed basis.

- The grammar challenges can be completed individually, with a partner, or as a class.

- Students may complete challenges at home or in the classroom.

- Instructors can provide guided feedback upon completion, or ask students to self-correct or peer-edit. All exercises are formatted to provide for ease of correction and assessment.

- The *Grammar Challenge 5* answer key is available to teachers on the *Stand Out* Web site at: **standout.heinle.com**. It can be printed out for student use.

- The grammar challenges need not be followed in any particular order within a unit. Some challenges will be review for students, while others will reinforce the newer structures from *Stand Out 5 Student Book*.

- The *Stand Out 5 Grammar Challenge* workbook is an effective supplement in a multi-level classroom because it challenges the highly motivated students while providing support for students who need extra reinforcement.

The appendix includes a glossary of grammar terms with examples. This is intended as a reference for both students and teachers, but it is not intended that all these terms will be understood at this level. The appendix also includes grammar charts from the *Stand Out 5 Grammar Challenge* workbook as well as lists of irregular verbs and verb conjugations.

However you choose to use it, you'll find that the *Stand Out 5 Grammar Challenge* workbook is a flexible and effective grammar tool for teachers and students seeking challenging grammar instruction.

Getting to Know You

CHALLENGE 1 ➤ Introductions

 Kenji  Anya  Gilberto Marie

A Imagine that you know these people. What would you write about them? Use your imagination!

Kenji: _____

Anya: _____

Gilberto: _____

Marie: _____

Introductions	
Introduction	**Responding to an Introduction**
I'd like to introduce you to Juan.	It's a pleasure . . . to meet you.
I'd like you to meet Peter.	. . . meeting you.
This is my friend, Ana.	(I'm) pleased to meet you.
Do you know Caroline?	(It's) . . . nice to meet you.
Have you met my brother, Zach?	. . . good to meet you.
I'd = *I would* Use *would* to show a preference. **Note:** In these cases, *would* is not associated with an *if*-statement: John would play soccer, and I prefer basketball.	In short common introductions with phrases and statements, it is appropriate in speaking to leave off the subject and the verb. The subject and verb are implied.

Simple Past/Present Perfect/Simple Present		
Simple Past	Something that started and ended in the past.	Juan was born in 1989.
Present Perfect	Something that started in the past and continues in the present.	Juan has been in the United States for three years.
Present	Something that is true about the present.	Juan works in a department store.
Future	Something that will happen in the future.	He is going to / will study architecture in college.

B Respond to each introduction. Use a different expression for each one.

EXAMPLE: *A:* I'd like to introduce you to my friend, Maddy.

        B: It's nice to meet you, Maddy.

1. *A:* This is my friend, Zhou.

   B: _____

2. *A:* Do you know Erin?

   B: _____

3. *A:* Have you met Chinh?

   B: _____

4. *A:* I'd like you to meet Enrique.

   B: _____

C Complete the sentences about each of the people using the verb and tense listed in parentheses.

EXAMPLE: Chinh is _____is_____ (be – *present*) a student.

1. Zhou _____ (be – *past*) born in China.

2. He _____ (live – *present*) in Texas now.

3. He _____ (move – *future*) to California in a few months.

4. Chinh _____ (come – *past*) from Vietnam five years ago.

5. Chinh _____ (be – *present perfect*) in school for two years.

6. She _____ (study – *future*) nursing once her English improves.

7. Enrique _____ (be – *past*) an engineer in Mexico.

8. He _____ (move – *present perfect*) three times since he came to the U.S.

9. He _____ (like – *present*) to see new places and meet new people.

10. He _____ (stop – *future*) moving so he can look for an engineering job.

D Imagine that you are meeting someone for the first time. Complete the conversation with appropriate phrases.

Zhou: I'd like you to meet my friend, Erin.

You: _____

Erin: What's your name?

You: _____

Erin: I'm actually from here. But I was born in Sweden. Where were you born?

You: _____

Erin: I came here fifteen years ago with my family. What about you?

You: _____

Erin: How interesting. It's so nice to have met you. I hope we see each other in school.

Getting to Know You

CHALLENGE 2 ➤ Conversation Strategies

Conversation Strategies

A Write four things you think the people below would be interested in doing. Then, compare your answers with another student.

Interests	Interests	Interests	Interests
1. _____	1. _____	1. _____	1. _____
2. _____	2. _____	2. _____	2. _____
3. _____	3. _____	3. _____	3. _____
4. _____	4. _____	4. _____	4. _____

Asking about Personal Interests	Responses
So, what do you like to do in your free time?	That's interesting.
What are your hobbies?	How fun!
What are your interests outside of school/work?	Wow, that's great.
Are you into music?	Me, too!
What do you like to do?	Not me, I . . .
What are your plans for the weekend?	Sounds like we have something in common.
What's your favorite movie?	

Conversations are more productive when:

- You ask about the person you are talking to.
- You take interest in the person you are talking to.
- You ask follow-up questions.

Other strategies:

- Learn to summarize what someone says when you don't understand.
- Learn to disagree politely showing respect for the other person's opinion.
- Learn to express yourself clearly and in a simple way.
- Learn to maintain eye contact.

B **Circle the best answer to each question.**

EXAMPLE: *Q:* So, what do you like to do in your free time?

A: (I like to go to the movies.) / No, not much.

1. *Q:* What are your hobbies?

   A: Reading books and fixing up old cars. / We're going to the mountains.

2. *Q:* What are your interests outside of school/work?

   A: I'm a carpenter. / Playing soccer and cooking.

3. *Q:* What do you like to do?

   A: I like fresh fruit and red meat. / I like to train for bike races.

4. *Q:* What are your plans for the weekend?

   A: Surfing and reading comic books. / I'm going to a family reunion.

C **Match the best response to each question and then write the conversation on the lines.**

a. __1__ I like to ride my bike in my free time.

b. _____ Yes, I'm usually training for a bike race.

c. _____ I like to have fun while I'm exercising.

d. _____ That sounds like fun. I wish I lived near some good trails.

1. What do you like to do in your free time?

   I like to ride my bike in my free time.

2. Why do you sing when you exercise?

   _____

3. I've heard that hiking is both exciting and healthy. What do you think?

   _____

4. Is it true that you spend a lot of time riding your bike?

   _____

D **Answer the following questions about yourself.**

1. What do you like to do in your free time? _____

2. Are you into sports? _____

3. What are your plans for the weekend? _____

4. What's your favorite type of music? _____

E **Now ask your partner the same questions and write his or her answers below.**

1. _____   2. _____

3. _____   4. _____

Conversation Strategies

PRE-UNIT

Getting to Know You

CHALLENGE 3 ➤ Editing

 A There are ten mistakes in Andrea's letter. Circle each mistake you find.

Dear Alexi,

    I am so anxious to see you. I can't wait for your visit in (july) We will having a great time. I want to show you my new school, we learning a lot of interesting things. My english is improving. This school private is great. I am preparing for work in the busness feild. I will meet you at the bus stop at 4:00 on monday.

Your friend always,

Andrea

 B Talk with a partner. Can you fix the mistakes in Andrea's letter above?

Editing	
Capitalization	Capitalize every proper noun.
	Capitalize the first letter of the first word of every new sentence.
Spelling	Check spelling in a dictionary or ask a friend.
Nouns	Check to make sure nouns are written correctly, singular or plural.
Verbs	Verbs should agree with the noun and be in the correct tense.
Word order	Make sure subjects in statements come before the verb and that adjectives come before the noun they describe.
Punctuation	Every sentence should end with a period, exclamation point, or question mark. Separate series (three or more adjectives, or nouns) with commas.

C Now look back at the letter you corrected. Decide what type of mistakes you corrected.

D Underline the correct sentence. Edit the incorrect sentence. On the line, write the type of mistake using the terms from the chart on the previous page.

EXAMPLE: <u>Last Monday, I registered for classes at my new school.</u>

last monday, I registered for classes at my new school. ___capitalization___

1. The bookstore sell books for al the classes.

   <u>The bookstore sells books for all the classes.</u> _____

2. Have you ever been to art museum on campus?

   <u>Have you ever been to the art museum on campus.</u> _____

3. No, but I did go to local exhibit art that came to town.

   <u>No, but I did go to the local art exhibit that came to town.</u> _____

4. Last week, she met with the guidance counselor.

   Last week, she met with the giudance counslor. _____

5. The counselor told her that she should take some harder class.

   <u>The counselor told her that she should take some harder classes.</u> _____

E Correct the mistakes in each sentence.

EXAMPLE: Chinh looked at many ~~school~~ before she chose the best one for nursing.
                                        schools

1. she was looking for one with the best teachers?

2. She got great recomenations from the teachers at her previus school.

3. She hope to complete her degree in three yeas.

4. She is going to moves so she can be closer to her new school

5. chinh will have to work at night so she can pays for school.

6. She have a time-part job as a server food in a restaurant.

F Imagine that you are Chinh writing a letter to Jason, a friend you met at your last school. Write a personal letter, including all of the information from the exercise above.

Editing

Balancing Your Life

CHALLENGE 1 ➤ Gerunds as Objects of Prepositions

Gerunds as Objects of Prepositions

A Read the paragraphs. Describe the type of learner using the descriptions in the box. The first one has been done for you.

visual/spatial	verbal/linguistic	~~logical/mathmatical~~
body/kinesthetic	musical/rhythmic	

1. Marion likes to make connections between what she has heard before and what she is learning at the moment. She often tries to put things in categories. She analyzes all the information before she completely understands new concepts. Marion is a
   _____logical/mathematical_____ learner.

2. Neda is always singing. Sometimes the teacher asks her to sing to herself because she can start singing very loudly and doesn't even know it. She tries to be quieter but then she begins to tap out rhythms on her desk with her fingers. Neda is a
   _____ learner.

3. Mario needs to see what he is learning. Listening to information is not enough. When he listens to the teachers or finds out about new information, he tries to draw it. He often makes graphs and charts to help him understand better. Mario is a
   _____ learner.

4. Cynthia likes to discuss new information with her friend in class. She often repeats what the instructor says to her friend. When she does this, she understands it much better. Cynthia is a
   _____ learner.

5. Jim and John are always interested in moving around in the room. They don't mind changing positions and trying to act out what is being discussed. Jim and John are
   _____ learners.

Gerunds as Objects of Prepositions			
Verb	**Preposition**	**Gerund**	**Example sentence**
learn learn best	by	writing participating	He **learns by writing** everything down. They **learn best by participating** in a discussion.
learn	through by	repeating watching	They **learn through listening**.
practice	by	relating solving	We **practice by repeating** what we hear. I **practice by watching** a video.
(be) good	at	remembering	Logical learners **are good at solving** problems.
excel	in	taking	You **excel in remembering** information.
succeed	in	listening	I **succeed in taking** good notes.
struggle	with	identifying	That student **struggles with listening** in class.

B Complete each sentence with the correct forms of verbs and gerunds.

EXAMPLE: Mehry _____learns_____ (learn) best by _____taking_____ (take) detailed notes.

1. I always _____ (struggle) with _____ (solve) math problems.

2. They _____ (be) really good at _____ (remember) what they've heard.

3. His teacher _____ (excel) at _____ (explain) ideas clearly.

4. Peter _____ (practice) by _____ (repeat) facts out loud.

5. Kim and her study partner _____ (learn) by _____ (participate).

6. He _____ (be) not good at _____ (relate) to other students.

C Circle the correct preposition.

EXAMPLE: She practices (in /(by)) drawing pictures.

1. He succeeds (in/with) remembering obscure facts.

2. They struggle (by/with) taking clear notes.

3. She learns (by/at) memorizing the notes she has taken.

4. Therese is good (in/at) identifying scientific solutions.

5. I practice math (by/with) solving five problems every night.

D Look back at the people from Exercise A. Write a sentence to describe each person. Try to use a different verb and gerund for each statement you write.

EXAMPLE: Marion _____practices by putting things in categories_____.

1. Neda _____.

2. Mario _____.

3. Cynthia _____.

4. Jim and John _____.

E Write two sentences to describe your learning style.

EXAMPLE: I struggle with memorizing new concepts.

1. _____

2. _____

UNIT **1**

Balancing Your Life

CHALLENGE 2 ➤ Future Conditional Statements

 Discuss the different educational goals in a group. What are they and how long does it take to earn each one?

> High School diploma or GED Certificate
> Associate of Arts degree (AA)
> Bachelor's degree (BA or BS)
> Master's degree (MA or MS)
> Doctorate (PhD)

B Make a list of one job or career for each type of diploma, certificate, or degree.

Job or Career	Diploma/Certificate/Degree

Future Conditional Statements		
If-clause (condition) *if* + subject + present tense verb	**Future statement (result)** subject + *will* + base verb	**Example sentence**
if she gets a master's degree	she will make more money	**If** she gets a master's degree, she will make more money. She will make more money **if** she gets a master's degree.
if he is good at computations	he will do well with computers	**If** he is good at computations, he will do well with computers. He will do well with computers **if** he is good at computations.

- The future statement is dependent on whether or not the *if*-clause happens or not.
- The *if*-clause cannot stand alone.
- The *if*-clause can come first or second. When the *if* clause comes first, use a comma.
- When the *if*-clause follows the future statement, don't use a comma.
  > She will make more money *if* she gets a master's degree.

C **Circle the condition. Underline the result.**

EXAMPLE: <u>I will go</u> to school full time (if I save) enough money.

1. If she passes the bar exam, she will practice law in Texas.

2. I will look for a job as a dental assistant if I get my certificate.

3. If Emil doesn't get into the university, he will go to a community college and then transfer.

4. If she wants to be a doctor, she will have to go to medical school.

5. He will have to look for investors if he wants to start his own business.

6. If Sasha gets an internship at that company, they will pay for her to go to school.

D **Correct each statement.**

                        goes
EXAMPLE: If Maya ~~go~~ to technical school, she will get a better job.

1. Mario will have to get another job if he want to pay for college.

2. If Elias moves out of the city, he will finding better job opportunities.

3. If we finished our degrees in three years, we can start working sooner.

4. Kendra will application to several more schools if she doesn't get into her first choice.

5. She will ask her boss to change her hours is she get accepted at the technical school.

6. Will you apply for scholarships if you went to the university?

E **Complete each statement with a condition or a result.**

EXAMPLE: If I don't pass the entrance exam, _____<u>I will study harder and take it again.</u>_____

1. If I get into college, _____.

2. I will get a better job _____.

3. I will make more money _____.

4. If I quit my job, _____.

UNIT 1 Balancing Your Life

CHALLENGE 3 ➤ Simple Tenses: Past, Present, and Future

A **Read about Andre.**

I have a busy life. My family is the most important thing to me. My family is the reason I work a lot. I work so much because I need to make money so I can support them. I have to travel for my job every week, so I see my wife, two children, and my dog only on the weekends. When I am home, I am tired so I sleep a lot. Before I had this job, I didn't travel and I worked from home. It was a good job, but I needed to make more money to pay for all our new expenses. When I get my promotion, I will work less. I will work from the office only three miles from my house. I will work hard now so I can slow down in the future.

B **Discuss Andre's paragraph. Answer the questions below.**

1. What does Andre say is most important to him? Do you agree? What do you think his wife and children think?

2. Do you think Andre will work fewer hours after he gets a promotion? Why or why not?

Simple Tenses				
Subject	**Past**	**Present**	**Future**	
I	spent	spend	will spend	more time with my brothers.
You	enjoyed	enjoy	will enjoy	being a mother.
He, She, It	studied	studies	will study	English every day.
We	put	put	will put	our studies first.
They	worked	work	will work	too many hours.

Be			
Subject	**Past**	**Present**	**Future**
I	was	am	will be
you	were	are	will be
he, she, it	was	is	will be
we	were	are	will be
they	were	are	will be

C Complete each sentence with the correct form of the verb *study*.

EXAMPLE: Next year, I _____will study_____ math.

1. Last week, I _____ with a new partner.

2. He _____ at the library every day.

3. Next week, they _____ for their final exams.

4. She never _____ by herself.

D Complete each sentence with the correct form of the verb *work*.

1. We always _____ on the weeknights.

2. Two years ago, I _____ over 50 hours a week.

3. Yesterday, he _____ a short shift.

4. You _____ at night next week so you can be home with your kids during the day.

E Complete each sentence with the correct form of the verb *be*.

1. I _____ always trying to do better at my job.

2. She _____ still in school last year.

3. He _____ never late to English class.

4. Next month, I _____ taking a higher level class.

F Complete the paragraph with an appropriate form of one of the verbs in the box. Some verbs may be used more than once.

be	want	take	get	look	need	have

Right now I _____am_____ a student. I study history and political science. One day I _____ _____ a teacher and teach in high school so I _____ to get my special subjects teaching credentials. My classes _____ really hard and I _____ to study for at least three hours every night. Last year, I _____ easier classes so I _____ able to work and go to school at the same time. But this year, I _____ only going to school. I _____ my bachelor's degree at the end of next year and then I _____ to take classes for my credentials. That _____ about a year. Hopefully, I _____ able to pass the credential exams and then I _____ for a job as a teacher.

Balancing Your Life

UNIT 1

CHALLENGE 4 ➤ Past Perfect

A Look at the events in Eva's life. Number the events from 1 to 9 in the order they most likely occurred. The first event is numbered for you. Compare and discuss your answers with other students.

_____ She got a job as a waitress speaking English.

_____ She got a job with a local newspaper.

_____ She graduated from the university.

__1__ She learned English in an adult school.

_____ She sold a book to a publisher.

_____ She studied journalism.

_____ She took classes at a two-year college.

_____ She went to a university.

_____ She wrote a book of English poems.

B Write _true_ or _false_ in front of each statement.

1. _____ Eva had learned English before she got a job as a waitress.

2. _____ Before she went to a two-year college, she had gone to a university.

3. _____ After she had studied journalism, she wrote a book of English poems.

4. _____ She had gotten a job with a local newspaper before she graduated.

Past Perfect				
Subject	_Had/Hadn't_	**Past participle**	**Complement**	**Clause**
I, he, she, we, you, they	had hadn't	trained	for six months	before I ran the marathon
		(already) **taken**	English classes	when I started college
		studied	at the university	I went to medical school*
*_After_ I **had studied** at the university, I **went** to medical school.				
• The past perfect can show an event that happened before another event in the past. • The past perfect can show that something happened before the verb in the _when_ clause. *The past perfect can show something that happened after another event. In this case the _after_ clause includes the past perfect and the clauses are separated with a comma.				

C **Underline what happened first.**

EXAMPLE: <u>After I had studied computer science,</u> I got a job as a programmer.

1. Gabe had worked as a mechanic before he went to technical school.

2. When I got my degree, I had already been teaching for five years.

3. Kevin learned how to use a computer after he had graduated from high school.

4. Before they applied to college, they had studied English for three years.

D **Complete each sentence with the correct form of the verb.**

EXAMPLE: After she _____*had started*_____ (start) her own cleaning business, she

_____*went*_____ (go) to business school.

1. Before you _____ (finish) school, you _____ (work) full time as a photographer.

2. She _____ (study) at an adult school for four years before she

_____ (apply) to college.

3. After Antonia _____ (find) a good school for her kids, she

_____ (began) to look for a school for herself.

4. Evan _____ already _____ (pick) a major when he

_____ (register) for his first year of school.

E **Take one idea from the first column and another idea from the second column and write past perfect sentences.**

~~get together a portfolio~~	apply for a job with a shipping company
ride four days a week	~~find an art school~~
work for the postal service	compete in a bicycle race
meet with a counselor	kids are born
save money for college	choose a college major

EXAMPLE: <u>I had gotten together my portfolio before I found an art school.</u>

1. _____

2. _____

3. _____

4. _____

F **Think about your own goals or things you have accomplished. Write two past perfect sentences.**

1. _____

2. _____

UNIT 1 Balancing Your Life

CHALLENGE 5 ➤ Future Perfect

Future Perfect *(sidebar)*

A Read Felipe's goals below. Which ones do you share?

1. Learn English.
2. Graduate from college.
3. Get married.
4. Have children.
5. Get a job that pays over $50,000 a year.
6. Buy a new house.

B List some obstacles that might keep Felipe from reaching the goals above.

Obstacles

1. Felipe is homeless.
2. _____
3. _____
4. _____
5. _____
6. _____

Future Perfect Tense				
Subject	*Will Have*	Past participle		Second future event (present tense)
I	will have	become	a teacher	by the time my kids are in school.
He	will have	been	a graphic designer (for five years)	when he turns 35.
They	will have	found	a job	by the time I finish school.

- We use the future perfect to talk about an activity that will be completed before another time or event in the future. **Note:** The order of events is not important. If the second future event comes first, use a comma.

  By the time my kids are in school, I will have become a teacher.

C) Match a goal with a time. Then, write the complete sentence below.

Goal

1. Sharon and Vu will have started their business
2. Sharon will have hired all the employees
3. Vu will have completed construction
4. They will have been open for six months

Time

a. by the end of the month.
b. when they turn 40.
c. when their kids graduate from high school.
d. by the time the doors open.

1. _Sharon and Vu will have started their business when they turn 40._
2. _____
3. _____
4. _____

D) Complete each sentence with the correct verb form.

EXAMPLE: By the time school _____starts_____ (start), Franco ____will have chosen____ (choose) a major.

1. He _____ (give) his notice at work before the first day of class _____ (begin).

2. Greta _____ (buy) a new computer before her first paper _____ (be) due.

3. By the time he _____ (complete) his first marathon, he _____ (run) over 250 miles.

4. When she _____ (turn) 50, she _____ (married) for over 25 years.

5. You _____ (look) at fifteen schools by the time you finally _____ (choose) one.

6. His father _____ (get) his high school diploma when his son _____ (graduate) from college.

E) Complete each statement.

EXAMPLE: By the time I have my degree, _I will have studied for more than eight years._

1. By the time I finish school, _____.
2. When I graduate from college, _____.
3. When I turn 70, _____.

Balancing Your Life

EXTENSION CHALLENGE 1 ➤ Gerunds as Direct Objects

A Look at the list of multiple intelligences. Check (✓) what you think describes you.

☐ visual/spatial   ☐ musical/rhythmic

☐ verbal/linguistic   ☐ interpersonal

☐ logical/mathematical   ☐ intrapersonal

☐ bodily/kinesthetic   ☐ naturalistic

B Describe why you checked the specific intelligences in Exercise A.

EXAMPLE: I chose "musical" because I enjoy listening to music.

Hint: Consider describing things you *prefer, enjoy,* and *like* to do.

_____

_____

_____

_____

_____

		Gerunds as Direct Objects	
Verb	**Infinitive or Gerund**	**Example sentence**	**Other verbs that follow the same rule**
want plan	+ infinitive	He **wants to study** art. He **planned to learn** English.	arrange, choose, decide, expect, hope, prepare, resolve
enjoy finish	+ gerund	She **enjoys fixing** cars. She **finished studying** for the test.	anticipate, consider, complete, discuss, imagine, necessitate, recommend
like	+ infinitive or + gerund	They **like to paint**. We **like painting**.	begin, commence, continue, love, prefer, try
infinitive = *to* + verb gerund = verb + *ing*			

C Circle the correct verb.

EXAMPLE: My sister is considering ((working) / to work) with computers.

1. We expect (completing / to complete) the project by May.

2. His parents recommended (asking / to ask) his counselor to suggest a career.

3. Finnian imagined (looking / look) for a college in California.

4. Erin enjoys (practicing / to practice) the violin early in the morning.

5. Miles and Connor hope (competing / to compete) in the water polo tournament.

6. The girls want (finding / to find) a franchise they can buy together.

7. He and his wife discussed her (changing / to change) careers so she can stay home with the kids.

8. She never anticipated (loving / to love) her job as much as she does.

D From the chart on the previous page, choose a verb to complete each sentence. More than one verb may be possible.

EXAMPLE: The chef _____prefers_____ to cook vegetables.

1. We _____ to live near the city when we finally buy a house.

2. He _____ changing careers so he could become a designer.

3. They _____ looking for more ways to spend time together as a family.

4. She _____ working night shifts so she could pursue her teaching degree during the day.

5. Her family _____ to move back to their country.

6. Christa's son _____ taking things apart and putting them back together.

E Complete each sentence.

EXAMPLE: My teacher recommended _____reading for 30 minutes each night._____

1 I enjoy _____.

2. My family hopes _____.

3. I never expected _____.

4. I discussed _____.

5. My friend is preparing _____.

6. I have always considered _____.

UNIT 1

Balancing Your Life

EXTENSION CHALLENGE 2 ➤ Future Perfect Continuous

A Complete the chart with your career goals. Decide on a timeline.

GOALS   Completion Date

Long-Term Goal:		
Short-Term Goal 1:		
Short-Term Goal 2:		
Short-Term Goal 3:		

B Use the future perfect to write about your career goals.

EXAMPLE: <u>I will have finished school by the time I start my second job.</u>

_____

_____

_____

_____

Future Perfect Continuous: *Will have been* + Verb + *ing*		
Example sentence	**Duration**	**Future event or action**
She **will have been studying** architecture for three years by the time she gets her degree.	three years	gets her degree
They **will have been working** at the same job for twenty years when they retire.	twenty years	retire

- Use the *future perfect continuous* to emphasize **the duration** of an activity that leads up to a future time or event.

Note: The *future perfect* is used in a similar way, but it doesn't emphasize duration.

C **Complete each sentence with the correct form of the future perfect continuous.**

EXAMPLE: She ___will have been working___ on the same project for over two years at the end of this month.

1. He _____ (study) English for four years by the time he goes to college.

2. Tina _____ (writing) her first novel for three years by the time it is completed.

3. I _____ (do) the same job for six months when I get a promotion.

4. Paul _____ (prepare) to get his architecture license for over six years when he takes his final exam.

5. They _____ (drive) the same car for over ten years before they finally buy a new one.

6. Chinh _____ (help) her family with their business for fifteen years before starting her own business.

D **Choose one part from each column below and write complete sentences.**

I	II	III
~~They will have been working~~	for ten years	by the time she wakes up.
She will have been sleeping	for over five weeks	~~when they retire.~~
He will have been living there	for at least two years	before he gets furniture.
We will have been looking for a good school	~~for twenty-five years~~	by the time we find one.
I will have been playing	for twelve hours	before I buy a new guitar.

EXAMPLE: They will have been working for twenty-five years when they retire.

1. _____

2. _____

3. _____

4. _____

E **Think about three things you have been doing for a long time. Write sentences using present perfect continuous to describe those actions.**

1. _____

2. _____

3. _____

Personal Finance

CHALLENGE 1 ➤ Future Perfect vs. Future Perfect Continuous

A Tuba is 22 years old and depends on her parents to help her financially. She doesn't speak English yet, but she has a high school diploma and is making plans. Here are her goals.

I have many goals that are very important to me. First of all, I want to become financially independent. But before I do that, I need to pay off my credit cards. Right now I work two jobs to pay rent on a small apartment downtown and I have to pay $200 a month for the minimum balance on my credit cards. Unfortunately, I don't save any money. So, starting today I will begin to save and I will stop impulse buying. If I save $300 a month, I will have paid off my credit cards by the time I am 25. I also plan to pay off my car. I need a better job so I'm going to learn English and get a college degree. I'd like to become a nurse. By the time I turn 30, I will have a career and make a good living.

B Predict how long it might take Tuba to reach her goals.

Goal	Length of time
stop impulse buying	
pay off her credit cards	
pay off her car	
finish school and get degree	
start a career	

Future Perfect Tense	
Completed future event	**Second future event**
I **will have saved** $3,000	by the time he arrives.
You **will have paid** off the house	when you reach retirement.
They **will have found** jobs	by the time they finish school.

We use the **future perfect** to talk about an activity that will be completed before another time or event in the future.

Future Activity	Length of time	Second Future Event
I **will have been saving**	for three years	by the time he arrives.
You **will have been paying**	for 30 years	when you reach retirement.
They **will have been looking** for jobs	for 4 years	by the time they finish school.

- We use the *future perfect continuous* to talk about an activity that will be completed before another time or event in the future. However, in future perfect continuous the length of time is included.

Note: Sometimes either tense can be used and the meaning remains the same.

I will have lived in the house for thirty years by the time I move. I will have been living in this house for thirty years by the time I move.

C Decide which sentence in each pair is future perfect or future perfect continuous. Write *FP* (for future perfect) or *FPP* (for future perfect continuous) on the line.

EXAMPLE:

_FP___ *A.* I will have searched long and hard for a financial planner before I find one.

_FPP__ *B.* I will have been searching for a financial planner for six months by the time I find one.

_____ 1. *A.* He will have saved $5,000 for a car by the time he turns twenty.

_____ *B.* He will have been saving for eight years by the time he turns twenty.

_____ 2. *A.* You will have been looking for a computer for six months before you buy one.

_____ *B.* You will have looked all over for a computer before you buy one.

_____ 3. *A.* She will have been managing the household finances for more than fifteen years before she finally turns them over to her husband.

_____ *B.* She will have managed the household finances all by herself before she finally gives them over to her husband.

D Complete each sentence with future perfect or future perfect continuous (progressive).

EXAMPLE: At the rate you're going, I _____will have finished_____ (finish) my lunch before you have made your menu selections.

1. We _____ (pay) off our cars by the time we need new ones.

2. He _____ (start) contributing to college accounts for his kids by the time they are born.

3. You _____ (plan) your retirement party for months by the time you actually retire.

4. They _____ (look) for a house for six years by the time they can afford one.

5. I _____ (spend) thousands of dollars by the time I finish school.

6. My sister _____ (have) ten jobs before she finds the one she is happy with.

E Look at the predictions you made for Tuba in Exercise B. Write three sentences using the verb tense indicated.

EXAMPLE: FP _____Tuba will have stopped impulse buying in three months._____

1. FPP _____

2. FPP _____

3. FP _____

4. FPP _____

Personal Finance

CHALLENGE 2 ➤ Past Perfect Continuous

A Look at Sheila and Sam Nguyen's spending habits in the past and now. Which habits have improved? Which ones have gotten worse? Discuss with a partner.

In the past	Now
bought designer clothes	bargain shops
made coffee at home	buys coffee at a coffee shop
bought in bulk	buys things at the market when needed
spent every penny they made	have a savings account

B Make a chart showing your spending habits.

In the past	Now
1.	1.
2.	2.
3.	3.
4.	4.

Past Perfect Continuous Tense					
First past activity					**Second past event**
Subject	*Had*	*Been*	*-ing* verb		**Simple past**
Sheila	had	been	buying	designer clothes	before she started bargain shopping.
Sam	had	been	making	coffee at home	before he began buying it at a coffee shop.
They	had	been	paying	a higher deductible	before they called the insurance company.
We use the past perfect continuous to talk about an activity that was happening for a while before another event that happened in the past. For the more recent event, we use the simple past.					

C Circle the most recent past activity. Underline the prior past event.

EXAMPLE: She <u>had been spending her tips</u> before she decided to save up for a computer.

1. We had been paying cash for everything until we got credit cards.

2. Before he had a bank account, he had been saving his money in a drawer.

3. Lisa had been paying her bills by check every month until she started online banking.

4. I had been spending my whole paycheck until I started saving for retirement.

D Complete each sentence with the correct form of the past perfect continuous.

EXAMPLE: We _____had been living_____ (live) beyond our means before my wife lost her job.

1. Before Felipe rode his bike to work, he _____ (drive) an expensive car.

2. Margaret _____ (eat) dinner out every night before she started cooking at home.

3. My husband and I _____ (do) the finances together each month before I started doing them by myself.

4. Until you decided to lease a car, you _____ (make) payments to own your car.

5. We _____ (hire) babysitters a lot before we started taking the kids out with us.

E Look back at Sheila and Sam's spending habits. Write sentences using past perfect continuous.

EXAMPLE: <u>Sheila had been buying designer clothes before she started shopping for bargains.</u>

1. _____

2. _____

3. _____

F Look back at the chart your made in exercise B. Write sentences about your own spending habits, just like the ones you wrote for Sheila and Sam.

1. _____

2. _____

3. _____

4. _____

Personal Finance

CHALLENGE 3 ➤ Modals: *Can* and *Could* (Ability)

A Put a check (✓) in front of the things you *can* do.

1. _____ save money

2. _____ get a better job

3. _____ balance a checkbook

4. _____ pay bills online

5. _____ apply for a credit card

6. _____ invest in the stock market

B Discuss each of the above ideas with a partner. What do you need in order to be able to do each of them?

EXAMPLE: In order to save money, I need to have a job that pays me money and a place to save the money, like a savings account.

C Study the chart.

Modals: *Can* and *Could* (Ability)			
Subject	**Modal**	**Base**	**Complement**
I, you, he, she, it, we, they	can could	save invest spend	our money my savings his earnings

- Use *can* as a modal to express ability or what is possible to do. Use *could* with the same verb to express a suggestion or a possibility.

  We can invest our money in a CD. (expresses ability)

  We could invest our money in a CD. (expresses ability but only as a suggestion)

D Read each statement and decide if an ability or a possibility is being described. Bubble in the correct circle in front of *can* or *could*. Sometimes, both answers are possible, but choose the one that you think fits best.

EXAMPLE: I've seen you do a budget before so I know you _____ do it. ● can ○ could

1. I know you don't have very much in savings but you _____ open a CD. ○ can ○ could

2. She _____ get a second job if she wanted to. ○ can ○ could

3. We finally have enough money saved so now we _____ start a college fund for the boys. ○ can ○ could

4. You _____ meet with a financial planner if you want to get some advice about your finances. ○ can ○ could

5. He _____ start buying things online but he is afraid of his credit card number getting stolen. ○ can ○ could

6. Jarek just received his checkbook in the mail so now he _____ start writing checks. ○ can ○ could

E Complete each statement with *can* or *could* and a verb from the box.

invest	give	help	pool	tell	~~look~~	use

EXAMPLE: I _____ can look _____ for ways to save more money at home.

1. Jess _____ the computer to do her budget.

2. Derek _____ his money in his friend's restaurant.

3. We _____ our savings to charity.

4. _____ you _____ me reconcile my checking account?

5. _____ you _____ me what bank you use?

6. We _____ our resources and buy the couch together.

F Think about your own personal finances and look back at the ideas in exercise A. Using those ideas or some of your own, write two sets of statements using *can* and *could*.

EXAMPLE: I have been saving money so I can invest in the stock market. I could look for a financial advisor to give me some ideas on what to invest in.

1. _____

_____

2. _____

_____

Personal Finance

CHALLENGE 4 ➤ Modals: *Should* and *Ought to* (Advisability)

A Discuss the different ways to obtain credit. Number them from the easiest ways to the most difficult. Number 1 is the easiest.

_____ open bank accounts

_____ get and study your credit report

_____ fix your credit report

_____ apply for a bank credit card

_____ apply for a gas credit card

_____ apply for a department store credit card

_____ apply for a major credit card

_____ take out a small loan from your bank

B Work with a partner. Imagine that your partner needs to build up his or her credit. Give him or her some ideas.

EXAMPLE: You should apply for a bank credit card.

C Study the chart.

Modals: *Should* and *Ought to* (Advisability)			
Subject	**Modal**	***have* + participle**	**Complement**
I, you, he, she, it, we, they	**should** **ought to**	have looked	for errors
		have checked	our credit report

- Use *should* or *ought to* interchangeably. When used with *have* and the past participle, they express advice about something done in the past.

D Change each statement to past tense.

EXAMPLE: You should order your credit reports.

You should have ordered your credit reports.

1. You should check your statement. _____

2. He ought to call the bank. _____

3. They should find a lower interest rate. _____

4. I should start banking online. _____

5. We ought to consolidate our credit cards. _____

6. I should put money into an IRA. _____

E Change each statement to present tense.

EXAMPLE: You should have looked for an account with no fee.

You should look for an account with no fee.

1. He should have gotten his credit report. _____

2. We shouldn't have ignored the creditors. _____

3. They ought to have canceled their high interest cards. _____

4. I should contribute more to my 401K. _____

F Look at the ideas in Exercise A. Which ones should you do? Write statements.

EXAMPLE: I should apply for a department store credit card so I can save 10%.

1. _____

2. _____

3. _____

G Look back at the ideas in Exercise A. Which ones should you have done?
Write statements.

EXAMPLE: I should have fixed my credit report a long time ago.

1. _____

2. _____

3. _____

UNIT  **Personal Finance**

CHALLENGE 5 ➤ Modals: *May, Might,* and *Could* (Uncertainty)

A Read the situations below. What might be a possible reason for each problem? List some ideas about what you might be able to do about it.

1. A creditor calls you and tells you that you owe them $5,000. You have never dealt with the company before.

   _____

   _____

   _____

2. Your credit report lists three loans that are not yours.

   _____

   _____

   _____

3. Your bank account has five dollars in it instead of $500.

   _____

   _____

4. Your phone bill is twice as much this month.

   _____

   _____

   _____

Modals: *May, Might,* and *Could* (Uncertainty)			
Subject	**Modal**	***have* + participle**	**Complement**
it	may	have gotten	stolen online
someone, he, she, they	might	have found	your social security number
it	could	have been	identity theft

- Use modals like *may, might,* and *could* with *have* and the past participle to describe possibility or uncertainty in something that happened in the past.

   It could have been identity theft. (The speaker doesn't know. He or she is expressing the possibility. He or she is uncertain of what really happened.)

Unscramble the words to write statements of uncertainty.

EXAMPLE: have / could / a bank error / been / it ___It could have been a bank error.___

1. your credit card / you / have / might / at the hotel / left

_____

2. could / he / have / gotten / from an online site / your number

_____

3. have / your credit report / checked / may / they

_____

4. seen / they / have / your social security number / might

_____

C **Choose a modal *(may, might, could)* and write the correct form of the verb in each statement below.**

EXAMPLE: You _____might have forgotten_____ (forget) to shred your credit card statements.

1. She _____ (give) them a fake social security number.

2. They _____ (find) your bank account number.

3. Someone _____ (take) your driver's license from your wallet.

4. It _____ (be) identity theft.

D **Come up with possible explanations for each problem.**

EXAMPLE: Your electricity bill is $100 more than last month.

___I might have forgotten to turn the air conditioning off at night.___

1. You receive a package in the mail with your address but someone else's name on it. You didn't order the package.

_____

2. Your checking account has $2,000 more than it should.

_____

3. Someone calls your house asking for someone who doesn't live there.

_____

4. There is a charge on your credit card bill that you didn't make.

_____

UNIT 2 Personal Finance

EXTENSION CHALLENGE 1 ➤ Future Continuous

(A) **Read the paragraph and study the agreement.**

Brannigan is a financial counselor. He helps young couples that are just starting out manage their money and get out of debt. Many engaged couples spend more than they have on their weddings and honeymoons. Some have substantial loans and credit card debt. He helps people find ways to quickly reduce debt and avoid falling into greater financial hardships. He makes an agreement with them that includes things he promises to do as well as what he expects from his clients.

Our Agreement	
What you will do	**What I will do**
You will make a list of all your assets together as a couple or family.	I will place a value on your assets based on your descriptions.
You will identify all expenditures.	I will help identify ways to save on current expenditures.
You will distinguish between *wants* and *needs*.	I will negotiate with loan agents to reduce debt.
You will prioritize your expenditures.	I will create a payment plan.
You will meet with your financial counselor once a month for the first three months.	I will counsel with you at every step of the process. While you are doing each step, I will meet with you to help.
You will follow your financial counselor's advice.	You are accountable for your money. I will give you advice. It is your responsibility to follow the advice.

(B) **Discuss the questions.**

1. What is *substantial* debt?
2. What are *needs* and *wants?*
3. What are some examples of *assets?*
4. Do you think Brannigan's agreement is a good one? Why or why not?

Future Continuous	
Example	**Rule**
We **will be working** on the budget **when the financial planner arrives**.	to show when an action (simple present) interrupts a continuous action in the future (future continuous)
At 8:00 A.M. we **will be working** on the budget.	to express an action at a specific time in the future—an action that started before that time
We **will be working** on the budget while **you are talking** on the phone.	to show when two continuous actions will be happening at the same time in the future
Note: The future tense cannot be used in clauses. Therefore in the first example, we use the simple present and in the third example, we use the present continuous.	

C Complete each statement with the correct verb tenses.

EXAMPLE: He _____will be looking_____ (look) for ways to save money while she

_____pays_____ (pay) bills.

1. They _____ (meet) with a bank representative at 9 A.M.

2. She _____ (set) up her online bill paying when school

_____ (start).

3. Monica _____ (search) for a lower interest credit card while Jeff

_____ (find) a way to pay off their current cards.

4. At three in the afternoon, we _____ (discuss) our finances with
our new financial planner.

5. They _____ (refinance) their home while their friends

_____ (sell) the house they have lived in for twenty years.

6. You _____ (reconcile) your bank statement when I

_____ (get home).

7. I _____ (go) over my credit reports with a fine-tooth comb
tonight at 10 P.M.

8. They _____ (find) out their retirement options while their kids

_____ (start) to save for the future.

D Take one clause or phrase from each column and create sentences. Remember
to change the verb tenses to follow the rules of future continuous sentences.

EXAMPLE: He will be paying bills in the morning.

I	II
have a conference call	the loan officer arrives
review my credit statements	~~in the morning~~
go over the budget	watch TV
talk to the insurance company	at 7 P.M.
~~pay bills~~	file the bank statements
analyze the credit report	at four in the afternoon
meet with the bank manager	the meeting starts

1. _____

2. _____

3. _____

4. _____

5. _____

6. _____

Personal Finance

EXTENSION CHALLENGE 2 ➤ Future Modals: *Should, Ought to, May, Might,* and *Could* (Uncertainty)

A The following list includes ideas to avoid identity theft. Check (✓) the ones you might do.

☐ Don't purchase things online.

☐ Don't purchase things online without a secure connection to the internet.

☐ Check your credit report once a year.

☐ Check your credit report once a month.

☐ Never give out your social security number except to government agencies and employers.

☐ Don't give out personal information like driver's license numbers, bank account numbers, etc., to solicitors.

☐ Cancel unused credit cards.

☐ Shred all bills and statements after five years.

☐ Keep your wallet close to you at all times when in public.

B Prioritize the list of all the items in Exercise A from most important to least important by writing a number after each statement.

Future Modals: *Should, Ought to, May, Might,* and *Could* (Uncertainty)	
Example (modal + base verb)	**Rule**
He *should* **report** the identity theft. (He *shouldn't* **report** the identity theft.) He *ought to* **report** the identity theft. (He *ought not* **report** the identity theft.)	We use *should* or *ought to* to give a strong suggestion. However, we are uncertain if it will happen.
They *may/might/could* **check** his credit information once a month. (They *may/might/could* **not check** his credit information once a month.)	We use *may*, *might*, and *could* to show uncertainty about what will happen in the future. *May* is more certain than *might* or *could*.

C Take each statement from Exercise A and rewrite it using the given modal.

EXAMPLE: (should) <u>You shouldn't purchase things online.</u>

1. (may) _____

2. (ought to) _____

3. (could) _____

4. (should) _____

5. (might) _____

6. (could) _____

7. (may) _____

8. (should) _____

D Read each statement and write what you think should or may happen. Use *should, ought to, may, might,* or *could.*

EXAMPLE: He lost his wallet. <u>He should cancel his credit cards.</u>

1. She found a mistake on her credit card statement.

_____

2. His bank account is overdrawn.

_____

3. She left her ATM card in the ATM machine.

_____

4. They can't afford to pay their bills this month.

_____

E Think about your own financial situation. Write three statements about what you should or might do. Use *should, ought to, may, might,* or *could.*

EXAMPLE: <u>I should get copies of my credit reports.</u>

1. _____

2. _____

3. _____

Yes/No and Information Questions

Automotive Know-How

CHALLENGE 1 ➤ *Yes/No and Information Questions*

A Discuss the information below with a partner. Talk about the pros and cons of each car.

Year: 2004
Miles: 89,000
Mileage: 12 MPG
Upholstery:
cloth—fair condition
Additional Information:
GPS
antitheft device
new tires

Year: 2006
Miles: 45,000
Mileage: 14 MPG
Upholstery:
leather—good condition
Additional Information:
GPS

Year: 2007
Miles: 65,000
Mileage: 12 MPG
Upholstery:
leather—good condition
Additional Information:
GPS
antitheft device
Premium Stereo System

Yes/No and Information Questions	
Yes/No questions	
Past	Did the car **perform** well?
	Was it in an accident?
Present	**Does** it **have** airbags?
	Is it still under warranty?
	Are there any tears in the leather?
Future	**Will** it **pass** a smog check?
Present perfect	**Have** you **driven** the car cross-country?
	Has it **had** more than one owner?
Information questions	
Past	Where **did** you **buy** the car?
	Where **was** the damage?
Present	How often **do** you **change** the oil?
Future	How **will** you come up with a price?
Present perfect	How many owners **has** this car **had**?

B Fix the mistakes in the questions below.

                   been
EXAMPLE: Had it ~~be~~ in an accident?

1. Where is the license plates?

2. Have you ever replace the tires?

3. How often do you takes it in for service?

4. When was the last time you taken it in?

5. How many miles do it get to the gallon?

6. Will you allowing me to take it to my mechanic?

7. Have it been in an accident?

8. Are it in good condition?

C Look at the car advertisement. Write questions you might ask about the car using the question type and verb tense provided.

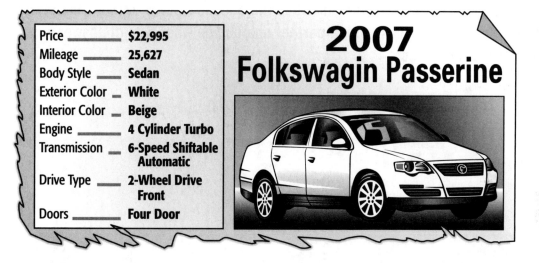

Price _____	$22,995
Mileage _____	25,627
Body Style ____	Sedan
Exterior Color _	White
Interior Color _	Beige
Engine _____	4 Cylinder Turbo
Transmission _	6-Speed Shiftable Automatic
Drive Type ____	2-Wheel Drive Front
Doors _____	Four Door

2007 Folkswagin Passerine

EXAMPLE: (y/n-present) <u>Does it have air-conditioning?</u>

1. (y/n-present perfect) _____

2. (info-future) _____

3. (info-present) _____

4. (info-present perfect) _____

5. (y/n-past) _____

6. (info-past) _____

D Practice asking your partner the questions you wrote. Have your partner make up answers.

Automotive Know-How

CHALLENGE 2 ➤ Question Words and Answers

A Answer the questions. (If you don't own a car, imagine you do.)

1. Who's your mechanic? _____

2. Where is your mechanic located? _____

3. How often do you rotate your tires? _____

4. When do you change your oil? _____

5. How do you pay for gas? (cash, credit card, etc.) _____

6. Why do you take your car in for repairs? _____

7. Whose car do you drive? _____

B Look back at the questions and underline the question words. Make a list of those words below. Then, discuss with a partner and decide what type of answer each question word requires.

Question Words
who

Answers
name of a person

Question Words and Answers			
	Question word	**Question**	**Sample answer**
Location	Where	is the fuel filter?	Next to the dipstick.
Choice	Which	mechanic do you use?	The one on First Street.
Location	Where	do you park your car?	On the street.
People	Who	repairs your car?	A mechanic.
	Whose	car is in the garage?	My brother's.
Time	When	do you change the oil?	Every 5,000 miles.
	How often	do you change the oil?	
Information	How	do you change the oil?	First, drain the oil.
	Why	do you change the oil?	Because the oil gets dirty.

C Match each question to an appropriate answer.

1. __f__ Who does your body work?   a. I have the mechanic do it.
2. ____ When do you replace your brakes?   b. About every 5 years.
3. ____ How do you change your oil?   c. Because our garage is full of stuff.
4. ____ Where is your gas tank?   d. My company.
5. ____ How often do you get a new car?   e. My sister's.
6. ____ Why do you park on the street?   f. The Body Shop in Acton.
7. ____ Whose car are you driving?   g. On the driver's side.
8. ____ Who pays for your car insurance? h. At 50,000 miles.

D Practice asking and answering the questions from Exercise C with a partner.

E Write a question that fits each answer below.

EXAMPLE: (my friend) Who sold you that car? _____

1. (every 2 years) _____

2. (my uncle) _____

3. (because it gets dirty from being parked outside) _____

4. (next to the grocery store) _____

5. (I like SUVs) _____

6. (every 3,000 miles) _____

F Write four questions to ask your partner about his or her car. Then, ask your partner the questions and write his or her answers below.

Question	Answer
1.	
2.	
3.	
4.	

Automotive Know-How

CHALLENGE 3 ➤ Negative Questions

A **Read the conversation.**

Amar: Naveen, could you loan me some money? I got into a car accident and I need to get my car fixed so I can get to work.
Naveen: Don't you have car insurance?
Amar: Yes, but it will take too long to get it fixed if I go through the insurance company.
Naveen: Didn't you call them?
Amar: No, not yet.
Naveen: Well, if you get it fixed on your own, they probably won't reimburse you.
Amar: But isn't that why I pay for the insurance?
Naveen: Yes, but they have to make an accident report and send a representative out to look at the damage. Then they will get estimates and decide how much they will pay to fix it.
Amar: Why didn't I just take the bus?

B **Look at the following pairs of sentences. What is the difference in structure and meaning? Discuss with a partner.**

1. Don't you have car insurance?   Do you have car insurance?

2. Didn't you call them?   Did you call them?

3. Isn't that why I pay for the insurance?   Is that why I pay for the insurance?

C **Study the chart.**

Negative Questions				
Auxiliary verb	Subject	Main verb	Information	Assumption
Don't	you	need	insurance?	She **needs** insurance.
Doesn't	she	have	uninsured motorist coverage?	She **has** uninsured motorist coverge.
Didn't	I	help	you fix your car?	I **helped** you fix your car.
Aren't	you		the principal driver?	You are the principal driver.
Isn't	she	driving	30 miles to work every day?	She is **driving** 30 miles to work every day.
Weren't	you	sitting	in the passenger seat?	You were **sitting** in the passenger seat.
We use negative questions when we assume that something is true.				

D Change each statement to a negative question.

EXAMPLE: She is covered by her husband's policy.
<u>Isn't she covered by her husband's policy?</u>

1. The insurance company is paying for the accident.

   _____

2. He has a policy that covers anyone who drives his car.

   _____

3. She called the insurance company five days ago.

   _____

4. They said they would look over the policy and get back to us.

   _____

5. Amar rented a car while his was being fixed.

   _____

6. I was driving when the stoplights went out.

   _____

E Read each statement and write an appropriate negative question.

EXAMPLE: She's driving a rental car. <u>Doesn't she have a car?</u>

1. They had to pay $3,200 to get their car fixed.

   _____

2. He just added his wife to his auto insurance policy.

   _____

3. We have a $1,500 deductible on our policy.

   _____

4. She doesn't have insurance for her new car yet.

   _____

5. The insurance agent called their house last week.

   _____

Automotive Know-How

CHALLENGE 4 ➤ Math Questions and Phrases

Trip	Odometer	Trip Miles	Gallons	MPG	Cost per Gallon	Cost per Mile
Start	66,101					
1	66,245	144	4.8	30	$4.75	.16
2	66,400	155	5.2	29	$4.77	.16
3	66,710	300	11	27	$4.73	.17
	AVERAGE	200	7	28.6	$4.75	.16

A Read Rodolfo's chart and answer the questions.

Look at Trip 1

1. How many miles to the gallon did Rodolfo get? _____

2. How many gallons did he put in his tank? _____

3. What was his odometer reading at the end of the trip? _____

Look at Trip 2

1. What was his odometer reading at the beginning of the trip? _____

2. What was his cost per mile? _____

3. What was his average MPG? _____

Look at Trip 3

1. How many miles did Rodolfo drive? _____

2. How many gallons did he put in his tank? _____

3. How much did he spend per gallon? _____

B Fill in the chart using the trip information in Exercise A.

Questions	Answers
How many miles did Rodolfo drive?	599 miles
How much gas did he put in?	
How much did he spend?	
What was the starting odometer reading?	
What were the average trip miles?	
What was the cost per mile?	
What is the average MPG?	
What was the ending odometer reading?	

C Imagine that a friend is asking you questions about a driving trip. Match each question to the correct answer.

1. _____ How much gas did you put in?   a. 45,987
2. _____ What was the cost per gallon?   b. 19 cents
3. _____ What was the odometer reading?   c. $4.33
4. __h__ How many miles did you drive?   d. 355 miles
5. _____ What were the average trip miles?   e. $46.87
6. _____ What was the cost per mile?   f. 12 gallons
7. _____ How much did you spend?   g. 24 mpg
8. _____ What is your average mpg?   h. 254 miles

D Unscramble the words to write questions. Then, choose an appropriate answer from the box.

~~16 gallons~~	about $60	about 19
15 cents	about 35,000 miles	about 230

1. much / gas / do / put / you / week / in / each / how

   Q: How much gas do you put in each week? _____   A: ____16 gallons____

2. miles / do / per / you / many / week / drive / how

   Q: _____   A: _____

3. odometer / right / what / your / is / now / reading

   Q: _____   A: _____

4. is / what / MPG / your

   Q: _____   A: _____

5. is / mile / cost / what / average / per / your

   Q: _____   A: _____

6. much / gas / do / on / spend / week / per / how / you

   Q: _____   A: _____

E Practice the questions above with a partner. Give your own answers.

UNIT 3 Automotive Know-How

CHALLENGE 5 ➤ Writing Questions

A Read the statements and decide if they are *true* or *false*.

1. _____ Teenagers have higher insurance rates than adults.

2. _____ Men are better drivers than women.

3. _____ Elderly people cause more accidents than middle-aged people.

4. _____ Bigger people can handle their alcohol better so they can drink and still drive.

5. _____ You should always warm up your car before you begin driving.

6. _____ You will be safe from a tornado if you stay in your car.

B Discuss your answers with a small group to see if you agree or disagree.

C Answer the questions based on the statements in Exercise A.

1. Who has higher insurance rates than adults? _____ teenagers _____

2. Who drives better than women? _____

3. Who causes more accidents than middle-aged people? _____

4. What can bigger people do? _____

5. What should you do before driving your car? _____

6. What will you be safe from if you stay in your car? _____

D Study the examples on how to write questions from statements.

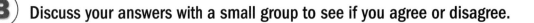

     when   how many

1. <u>During 2005</u>, <u>more than half</u> of the passengers ages 14 and younger died in a car crash

                 how

from <u>being in the car with a drunk driver</u>.

When/In what year did more than half of the passengers ages 14 and younger die in a car

crash from being with a drunk driver?

2. During 2005, *how many* passengers ages 14 and younger died in a car crash from being in a

car with a drunk driver?

During 2005, *how* did many passengers ages 14 and younger die?

E Underline the part of the sentence that answers each question.

EXAMPLE: (What?) Teens <u>have the lowest rate of seat belt use</u>, compared with other age groups.

1. (When?) From 1994 to 2003, a total of 57,142 teenagers were killed in motor vehicle crashes.

2. (How much?) Teenage drivers account for only 6.4 percent (12.5 million) of the total drivers in the United States.

3. (How many?) Teenage drivers account for 14 percent of all drivers involved in fatal crashes.

4. (Who?) Teenage drivers account for 18 percent of those involved in police-reported crashes.

F Take each statement and complete the questions based on the information given.

EXAMPLE: Alcohol-related motor vehicle crashes injure someone every two minutes.

      a. How often <u>do alcohol-related motor vehicle crashes injure someone</u>?

      b. What <u>injures someone every two minutes</u>?

1. Alcohol-related motor vehicle crashes kill someone every 31 minutes.

    a. How often _____?

    b. What _____?

2. During 2005, about 17,000 people in the U.S. died in alcohol-related motor vehicle crashes.

    a. What _____?

    b. When _____?

    c. How many _____?

3. In 2005, nearly 1.4 million drivers were arrested for driving under the influence of alcohol or narcotics.

    a. When _____?

    b. How many _____?

    c. What _____?

4. Drugs other than alcohol are involved in about 18 percent of motor vehicle driver deaths.

    a. What _____?

    b. How many _____?

Automotive Know-How

EXTENSION CHALLENGE 1 ➤ Tag Questions

A Answer the questions about yourself with a *yes* or *no*.

1. You have a car, don't you? _____

2. You didn't get in an accident, did you? _____

3. You are always driving the speed limit, aren't you? _____

4. You aren't parking in the handicap spaces, are you? _____

5. You will sell your car one day, won't you? _____

B Ask and answer the questions with a partner. Try to answer the questions using complete sentences.

EXAMPLE: *A:* You have a car, don't you?   *B:* Yes, I do.

Tag Questions		
	Negative statement + affirmative tag	**Affirmative statement + negative tag**
Past	He didn't sell his car, did he?	He sold his car, didn't he?
Past Perfect	You hadn't bought a car, had you?	You had bought a car, hadn't you?
Past Continuous	He wasn't driving, was he?	He was driving, wasn't he?
Present	She isn't the driver, is she?	She is the driver, isn't she?
Present Continuous	I wasn't driving the speed limit, was I?	I was driving the speed limit, wasn't I?
Present Perfect	He hasn't been drinking, has he?	He has been drinking, hasn't he?
Future	She won't take her car to work, will she?	She'll take her car to work, won't she?

- Tag questions are used to check if something is true or to ask for agreement.
- A tag question uses an auxiliary verb + a subject pronoun.
- The tag question uses the same tense as the main verb.
- Negative tags are usually contracted.

	Affirmative tag *(nobody, no one, nothing)*	**Affirmative statement + negative tag**
Past	Nobody wants an accident, do they?	Everybody knew the risks, didn't they?
Present	Nothing is more important, is it?	Everyone buys insurance, don't they?
Future	No one will buy it, will they?	Somebody will come, won't they?
	• Use *they* with *nobody, no one, someone, somebody, everyone,* and *everybody*.	
	• Use *it* with *nothing*.	

C Circle the correct tag question for each statement.

EXAMPLE: He will look for a new car, **doesn't he /(won't he?)**

1. You drive to work every day, **don't you / aren't you?**

2. She isn't carpooling anymore, **is she / isn't she?**

3. Nobody walks to school, **will they / do they?**

4. Gas has gotten expensive, **has it / hasn't it?**

5. I don't have time to pick you up, **don't I / do I?**

6. Hybrid cars have gone up in price, **have they / haven't they?**

D Complete each statement with the correct tag.

EXAMPLE: We have to have insurance, ___don't we?___

1. I have never applied for a car loan, _____

2. She didn't lease a new car, _____

3. They traded in their car, _____

4. No one will buy that car, _____

5. We won't be able to carpool in the morning, _____

6. You aren't parking in my parking space, _____

7. You hadn't given me a gas card, _____

8. They are seeing their car, _____

9. I have to pay for the accident, _____

10. She wasn't drinking, _____

E Think of a friend or family member who has a car and think of questions you could ask him or her. Come up with phrases to complete each tag.

EXAMPLE: _____This is your first car_____, isn't it?

1. _____, don't you?

2. _____, were you?

3. _____, hadn't you?

4. _____, have you?

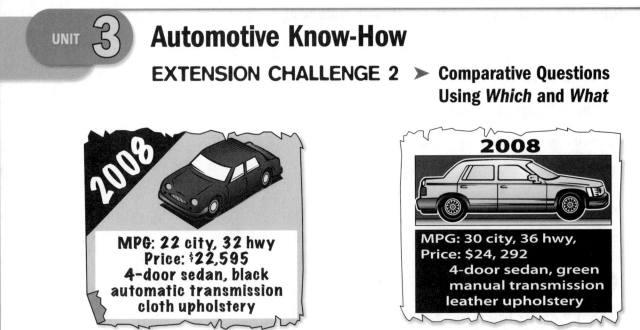

Automotive Know-How

EXTENSION CHALLENGE 2 ➤ Comparative Questions Using *Which* and *What*

UNIT 3

2008

MPG: 22 city, 32 hwy
Price: $22,595
4-door sedan, black
automatic transmission
cloth upholstery

2008

MPG: 30 city, 36 hwy,
Price: $24, 292
4-door sedan, green
manual transmission
leather upholstery

A Write questions you would like to ask the car dealer about the two cars.

_____

_____

_____

_____

Comparative Questions Using *Which* and *What*	
Example sentence	**Explanation**
Which car do you prefer, the black one or the green one? **Which** gets the best mileage? (which one)	Use *which* to compare and choose between two people or things or among a limited number of things.
What car is your favorite? (among all cars)	Use *what* to choose when there are many possible choices.

Among and *Between*	
Example sentence	**Explanation**
Which car do you want *between* the red and the black one?	Use *between* when you are comparing only two things.
What car is your favorite *among* the many in the showroom?	Use *among* when you are comparing more than two people or things.

B Choose *which* or *what* to begin each question.

	What	Which
EXAMPLE: _____ car do you prefer, the SUV or the sedan?	○	●
1. _____ color do you like best?	○	○
2. _____ type of seat do you prefer, cloth or leather?	○	○
3. _____ of the two is safer?	○	○
4. Of all the ones you've seen, _____ coupe is your favorite?	○	○
5. Between an automatic and standard shift, _____ do you prefer?	○	○
6. _____ one of the two drives the best?	○	○

C Choose *among* or *between* to complete each question.

	among	between
EXAMPLE: Which car do you like _____ the hybrids?	●	○
1. Which car do you prefer _____ all the ones you have driven?	○	○
2. Which is your favorite _____ the two?	○	○
3. What car would you buy _____ all the cars you've looked at?	○	○
4. _____ the sedan and the SUV, which is the safest?	○	○
5. What car did he like best _____ the five available?	○	○
6. _____ the ones for sale, which one gets the best gas mileage?	○	○

D Write questions about the ads using *which* or *what* and *among* or *between*.

MPG: 22 City, 32 Hwy
Price: $25,000
4-Door Sedan
White
Automatic Transmission
2008
Cloth Upholstery

MPG: 18 City, 25 Hwy
Price: $42,895
SUV
Blue
Automatic Transmission
2008, Cloth Upholstery

MPG: 30 City, 36 Hwy
Price: $28,687, Truck, Green
Manual Transmission
2008, Leather Upholstery

1. _____

2. _____

3. _____

4. _____

5. _____

6. _____

E Ask your questions to a partner.

Housing

UNIT 4

CHALLENGE 1 ➤ Causative Verbs: *Get, Have, Help, Make,* and *Let*

A The landlord usually inspects a recently vacated apartment. Look at his checklist. Whom would he call to fix each problem? Choose from the box below.

Apartment Inspection Checklist	
☐ paint is peeling ___painter___	
☐ holes in walls _____	
☐ plumbing leaks _____	
☐ ceiling leaks _____	painter
☐ electrical outlets don't all work _____	plumber
☐ dirty countertops _____	handyman
☐ dirty floors and walls _____	electrician
☐ dirty carpets _____	pest control
☐ insect infestation _____	building cleaning and maintenance company
☐ doors not hanging correctly _____	
☐ locks on windows not functioning ____	
☐ locks on doors not functioning ____	

B Using the information above, practice the following conversation with a partner, changing the underlined words.

A: Who will fix ___the peeling paint___?

B: The landlord will get ___a painter___ to come.

Causative Verbs: *Get, Have, Help, Make, Let*			
Subject	**Verb**	**Noun/Pronoun (object)**	**Infinitive (omit *to* except for *get*)**
He	will get	his handyman	to come.
She	had	her mom	wait for the repairperson.
The landlord	helped	me	move in.
Melanie	makes	her sister	pay half of the rent.
Mr. Martin	let	Melanie	skip one month's rent.

- Transitive verbs are verbs that require a direct object. Causative verbs are usually transitive verbs.

C Unscramble the words to write causative statements.

EXAMPLE: them / had / the handyman / under the mat / leave a key

<u>The handyman had them leave a key under the mat.</u>

1. the tenants / him / let / out front / put / a For Sale sign

   _____

2. made / my landlord / the holes in the wall / patch / me /

   _____

3. the landlord / for a month / us / will get / I / to give / free rent

   _____

4. her boyfriend / she / which couch to buy / decide / let

   _____

5. pay / my aunt / me / rent / helped / for a few months

   _____

D Choose a phrase from each column to write causative statements.

A	B	C	D
her parents	got	~~her friends~~	move in
his cousin	~~had~~	his tenants	pay an extra security deposit for the dog
I	have	my mom	pay one half the utilities
~~she~~	made	their friends	~~repair the damage they caused~~
the landlord	were helping	their neighbors	sleep on the couch for a few days
the renters	will let	us	to pay for the party

EXAMPLE: <u>She had her friends repair the damage they caused.</u>

1. _____
2. _____
3. _____
4. _____
5. _____

E Answer each question with a causative statement.

1. What did your parents help you do? _____

2. What does your teacher let you do? _____

3. What do your classmates get you to do? _____

4. What do you make yourself do? _____

Housing

CHALLENGE 2 ➤ Perception Verbs: *Feel, Hear, Listen to, Look at, Notice, Observe, See, Smell,* and *Watch*

(A) Look at the problems in an apartment for rent. Put them in the correct boxes below. Are they problems you *hear, see,* or *smell*?

Problems
- dirt
- insects
- insects in walls
- strange odor from carpet
- neighbors playing loud music
- leaky pipes
- holes in walls
- uncollected garbage

See

dirt

_____

_____

_____

Hear

_____

_____

_____

Smell

_____

_____

_____

Perception Verbs		
Subject + verb	**Direct object**	**Gerund or Base**
Simple Present		
I see / watch / look at	the landlord	fixing the sink.
I notice / observe	the gardener	clipping bushes on Tuesday.
I feel	the light switch in the dark.	
I hear / listen to	music	filling the room.
I smell	a strange odor.	
Simple Past		
I saw / watched / looked at	my neighbor	water (watering) the plants.
I noticed / observed	everything that went on there.	
I felt	the cold water	run (running).
I heard / listened to	noises	come (coming) from upstairs.
I smelled	a sweet smell.	

- Transitive verbs require a direct object. Perception verbs are usually transitive verbs.

- In the present tense, use the gerund if needed after the direct object. **Note:** In most of the examples above, the gerund is not needed. It just adds more information.

- In the past tense, use the base or gerund after the direct object.

Perception Verbs

B Choose a perception verb and complete each sentence. Use the verb tense indicated.

EXAMPLE: (past) They _____watched_____ the fire burn the apartment building across the street.

1. (present continuous) His mother _____ the emergency broadcast on the radio.

2. (future perfect continuous) We _____ the construction for three years by the time it is finished.

3. (past) I _____ the air-conditioning turn off.

4. (future) The landlord _____ at the entire apartment to see if it was cleaned properly.

5. (present perfect continuous) He _____ at that same house for sale for almost a year.

6. (present) I _____ music coming from the condo next door.

7. (past perfect) She _____ the gas before she called the gas company.

8. (past) Her husband _____ the unlocked door.

9. (present perfect) We _____ so many young tenants move into this building.

10. (future perfect) Her nephews _____ in by the time we get there.

C Complete each sentence with a direct object. Add a gerund or base verb if you need it to make your sentence clearer.

EXAMPLE: My neighbor smelled _____ the fire. _____

1. The teachers looked at _____.

2. Her uncle was watching _____.

3. She had been listening to _____.

4. Her brother had noticed _____.

5. We are looking at _____.

6. I observed _____.

7. She feels _____.

8. The realtor heard _____.

CHALLENGE 3 ➤ Relative Pronouns: *Who, That, When,* and *Where*

Relative Pronouns

A Read the letter that Jonathan wrote to his landlord.

June 23, 2008

Dear Mr. Michelson,

My name is Jonathan Appleby. My wife and I rent an apartment at 3765 West Birch Street. We have been at this residence for three years and faithfully pay the rent on time and keep our end of the rental agreement. I am writing this letter to document all of the problems that we are now facing in our apartment. This is our second letter to you. Please look over these issues as soon as possible.

First, the plumbing is becoming more of a problem every day. The leaking is getting worse. *The plumbing is one of the issues that I mentioned in my previous letter.* We wake up every morning with water on the bathroom floor coming from the sink. It is dangerous. My wife slipped yesterday. Fortunately, she was not injured, but I hope you will see that this problem is corrected within the next few days.

I also remind you of the time when we saw termites in the house. This is no longer a problem inside and the common areas are not our responsibility, but I have seen flying insects outside and I suspect they are termites. You may want to resolve this potential problem soon as well.

Finally, the handyman who came last week said that our carpet should be replaced. Have you heard from him? He sounded very definite about it. Our carpet is old from normal wear. It would be a great improvement if this could also be taken care of.

Thank you for your attention,

Jonathan Appleby

B What are the problems Jonathan mentions in his letter?

Types	Example sentence	Refers to
Things	The plumbing is one of the issues **that** I mentioned in my previous letter.	*that* refers to *plumbing*
Time	I remind you of the time **when** we saw termintes in the house.	*when* refers to *the time*
People	The handyman **who** came last week ...	*who* refers to *the handyman*
Place	That is a place **where** I would never live.	*where* refers to *a place*

- The phrases that begin with a relative pronoun are called *restrictive adjective clauses*.
- Restrictive adjective clauses give essential information about the noun they refer to. They cannot be omitted without losing the meaning of the sentence.

C Write the correct relative pronoun in each sentence.

EXAMPLE: Do you remember the time ____when____ we almost bought the house by the lake?

1. Did you ever find the lease agreement _____ I left on the counter?

2. He will never forget the time _____ he didn't get his security deposit back.

3. I want to look for a place in the city _____ you live.

4. Renting an apartment is one thing _____ I hope I will never have to do again.

5. She is the woman _____ found this apartment for us.

6. That is the apartment _____ they found the million dollars.

7. The painter _____ finished our house is a good friend of mine.

8. This is a house _____ I could live for the rest of my life.

D Match each statement with an appropriate adjective clause.

1. _____ She's renting the condo

2. _____ That's the landlord

3. _____ Can we find a time

4. _____ They are the friends

5. _____ I want to find a place

6. _____ That is one thing

a. who I was telling you about.

b. where I can have my two dogs.

c. where her parents used to live.

d. that I will never understand.

e. who helped me move into my new place.

f. when we can go over the lease together?

E Complete each statement with an adjective clause.

EXAMPLE: That is the place _where I want to live._ _____

1. She is the woman _____

2. This is the time _____

3. That is the thing _____

4. Will there ever be time _____

5. I really hope we can find a place _____

6. Did you see that man _____

Relative Pronouns

Housing

CHALLENGE 4 ➤ Passive Voice

Passive Voice

A The house below was improved over the years. Look at the list of improvements and the dates.

2235 Mockingbird Lane Lot 134

Date	Description
08-25-1974	built
09-20-1974	purchased ($86,000)
10-07-1974	yards landscaped
06-22-1985	pool added to backyard
09-15-1990	kitchen remodeled
10-10-1998	guest room added (150 square foot addition)
01-17-2004	sold/purchased ($452,000)

B What do you think contributed most to the improved value of the home? Discuss it with a group. Some ideas include:

☐ landscaping   ☐ inflation

☐ pool   ☐ neighborhood

☐ kitchen improvements   ☐ economy

☐ room addition

Passive				
Example sentence	**Passive subject**	**Be**	**Past participle**	**by + person (optional)**
The house was built in 1974.	The house	was	built	
The home will be insured by Home Mutual.	home	will be	insured	by Home Mutual
The bills are paid by the insurance company.	bills	are	paid	by the insurance company
It is estimated that the value of the home is $452,000.	it	is	estimated	

- Use the passive voice to emphasize the object of the action, or when the doer of the action is unknown or unimportant.
- To change an active sentence to a passive, switch the subject and the object, and change the verb to the correct tense of *be* + the past participle. The word *by* is used before the doer of the action.

C   **Circle the correct passive voice form.**

EXAMPLE: The construction site (will be cleaned) / will be clean up.

1. The new homes **be built / are built** with energy efficient heating and cooling.

2. The terms of the lease **can be found / can be find** on the landlord's website.

3. The condo **was sell / was sold** at the bottom of the market.

4. Her water heater **will be repaired / will repaired** by a handyman.

5. His bills **are being paid / are be paid** by the insurance company.

6. Homes for sale **can be lease / can be leased** until the owner finds a buyer.

D   **Change each active sentence to a passive one. Keep the verb tenses the same.**

EXAMPLE: The builders completed the house last month.

    The house was completed last month.

1. We added a second story after our kids were born.

2. The movers took all of our belongings to our new place.

3. The appraiser appraised our home last week.

4. The loan officer funded our loan before escrow closed.

E   **Write passive statements using the information from the chart in Exercise A.**

EXAMPLE: The house was built in August of 1974.

1.

2.

3.

4.

5.

6.

Housing

CHALLENGE 5 ➤ Future Passive

A There are several companies now that will help in the prevention of credit card theft. They do this by making several promises. Read the advertisement.

Prevent Identity Theft

Protect Yourself with THE IDENTITY SAFE

For $10 a month, we will:

- check your credit reports *every month for changes*
- alert you when changes appear
- renew fraud alerts on your credit *every three months*
- cancel all credit application offers *(junk mail)*
- provide suggestions to protect your credit in a *monthly newsletter*

If your identity is stolen, we will make it right, guaranteed!

B Discuss this offer with other students. It would cost $120 a year. You can do all of these things yourself with the exception of checking your credit report once a month for free. Is it worth the money?

Future Passive			
Example sentence	Subject	*will + be*	Past participle
Your credit report **will be checked** every month.	credit report	will be	checked
You **will be alerted** if there is something wrong with your report.	you	will be	alerted
Any credit offers **will be canceled**.	offers	will be	canceled
A newsletter **will be sent** to you every month.	newsletter	will be	sent

- The use of *will* is a common way to express the future passive.
- You may also use *be going to* but then it is more of a plan than a promise or commitment.

C Complete each statement with the correct future passive form of the verb given.

EXAMPLE: My credit report _____will be checked_____ (check) by the company.

1. I _____ (alert) if any changes appear on my credit report.

2. The fraudulent charges _____ (review) by the credit card company.

3. The banks _____ (notified) that she doesn't want any new credit card offers.

4. An annual report _____ (sent) to the clients.

5. Suggestions on how to reduce identify theft _____ (provide).

6. Any changes to your credit report _____ (identify).

7. The free copies of her credit reports _____ (mail) to her every three months.

8. The thief who stole his identity _____ (find).

D Complete each phrase with an appropriate verb. Use future passive.

EXAMPLE: The thief _will be caught._

1. The mistakes on her credit report _____.

2. His social security number _____.

3. A new credit card _____.

4. The bank that made the mistake _____.

5. The identify theft insurance _____.

6. The fraudulent charges _____.

E Think about services that your bank provides for you. Write four statements in the future passive describing those services.

EXAMPLE: _I will not be charged for my checks._

1. _____

2. _____

3. _____

4. _____

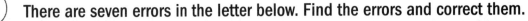

EXTENSION CHALLENGE 1 ➤ Business Letter Writing and Editing

A There are seven errors in the letter below. Find the errors and correct them.

June 28, 2008

Dear Mr. Gibbons,

This letter is to inform you that there is a problem with the apartment complex that must be repaired immediately. According to our lease agreement, you and Nestle management agency agreed to keep the common areas safe. We appreciate all you have done in this area, but there is still a lingering and potentialy problem serious.

based on my observations, one of the stone step leading up to the upper floor is broken. The third step from the top is chipped, and it is loose. This has repeatedly resulted in children the elderly and others tripping and injuring themselves. Fortunately, the injuries have been minimal, but you run the risk of serious injury, if this is not taken care of soon. I hope that you will see to this within the week.

Thank you,

Alexi Brashov

Alexi Brashov

B Make a list of problems you have experienced in your home or apartment.

_____ _____ _____ _____

Editing	
Capitalization	Capitalize every proper noun.
	Capitalize the first letter of the first word of every new sentence.
Spelling	Check spelling in a dictionary or ask a friend.
Nouns	Check to make sure nouns are written correctly, singular or plural.
Verbs	Verbs should agree with the noun and be in the correct tense.
Word order	Make sure subjects in statements come before the verb and that adjectives come before the noun they describe.
Punctuation	Every sentence should end with a period, exclamation point, or question mark. Separate series (three or more adjectives, or nouns) with commas.

C Find the errors in each sentence.

EXAMPLE: I'm ~~wiritng~~ **writing** this letter on behalf of all of the ~~resident~~ **residents** at Crystal ~~cove~~ **Cove**.

1. I'm writing these letter to complain about the security guard at our complex.

2. Sometimes at night, he isn't not in the booth where he is suppose to be.

3. Often times, I have see him let people in that don't lived here and aren't visit anyone who live here.

4. One of my visitor told me that he gave them the gate code so they could get in any time they wanted

5. In adition to all of these problems, he is not very freindly to the residents or their guest.

6. Please respond and let us know what you plans to do about this.

D Rewrite the sentences above in a paragraph format on a separate piece of paper.

E Identify each error. Some sentences may contain multiple errors.

EXAMPLE: she has never complained before. _____ capitalization _____

1. The managment company at her buildin rarely fixes things on time. _____

2. I think I will go to the meeting tonight. _____

3. All residents are invite to the meeting. _____

4. We have a list of all of the repairs that needs to be made. _____

5. We call day every and put in orders work. _____

F Write a letter to a landlord to complain about three different problems in your apartment. When you are finished, reread your letter and look for any errors. Write them below. Once you have finished, have a partner look at your letter and see if he or she can find any more errors.

Type of Error	Error	Correction
spelling	conversaion	conversation

UNIT 4 Housing

EXTENSION CHALLENGE 2 ➤ Comparative and Superlative Adjectives

Renter's Insurance QUOTE #1		Renter's Insurance QUOTE #2	
Value of Personal Property	$29,000	Value of Personal Property	$35,000
Deductible	$250.00	Deductible	$500.00
Liability	$100,000	Liability	$75,000
Medical Payments	$1,000	Medical Payments	$2,000
Annual Premium	$220.07	Annual Premium	$265.80
Monthly Payment	$18.34	Monthly Payment	$22.15

 Compare the two insurance quotes. Answer the questions.

1. Which one pays the least for medical payments?

2. Which one costs more, quote 1 or quote 2?

3. Which one has a higher deductible?

4. Which quote is better for you?

Comparative and Superlative Adjectives			
Type of adjective	Simple form	Comparative form	Superlative form
One-syllable adjectives	high	higher	the highest
One-syllable adjectives that end in -e	nice	nicer	the nicest
One-syllable adjectives that end in *consonant-vowel-consonant*	big	bigger	the biggest
Two-syllable adjectives that end in -y	pricey	pricier	the priciest
Other two-syllable adjectives	decent	more decent	the most decent
Some two-syllable adjectives have two forms	quiet friendly	quieter *or* more quiet friendlier *or* more friendly	the quietest *or* the most quiet the friendliest or the most friendly
Adjectives with three or more syllables	expensive	more expensive	the most expensive

- Use the comparative form to compare two things.
- If the second item is expressed, use *than*.
    My apartment is **bigger than** hers.
- Use the superlative form to compare one thing to two or more things.
- A prepositional phrase is sometimes used at the end of a superlative sentence.
    My automobile mechanic is the nicest repairman **in the business.**

	Simple Form	Comparative Form	Superlative Form
Irregular Adjectives	good	better	the best
	bad	worse	the worst
	far	farther	the farthest
	little	less	the least
	much/many	more	the most
Irregular Adverbs	well	better	the best
	badly	worse	the worst
	a little	less	the least
	a lot	more	the most

B Write comparative or superlative sentences. Use *than* when comparing two things.

EXAMPLE: my insurance company has / good rates

My insurance company has the best rates.

1. his deductible is / high _____

2. this estimate is / cheap / the first one we got _____

3. that company has / reputable service / our current one _____

4. her rate is / low / mine _____

5. your quote / expensive _____

6. my insurance company / good / online service _____

C Write comparative or superlative sentences using the words in parentheses.

EXAMPLE: He has a deductible. (low / his friend)

He has a lower deductible than his friend.

1. I have an apartment. (spacious / in my building)

_____

2. Before getting renter's insurance, you should compare quotes. (low / you can find)

_____

3. She is using an insurance agency that charges a fee. (high / of all the agencies)

_____

4. I plan to negotiate with the agent. (motivated / other agents)

_____

5. We found an insurance company. (decent / in the business)

_____

D Using the quotes on the previous page as a guide, come up with your own insurance quote. Now share with a partner and make comparative and superlative statements about your quotes.

Health

CHALLENGE 1 ➤ Adverbial Clauses of Place

A Think about where you would like to live if you could live anywhere. Check (✓) all the preferences that apply.

☐ I want to live where I can go running every day.

☐ I want to live wherever the mountains are nearby.

☐ I want to live anywhere I can see the ocean.

☐ I want to live anywhere there is no pollution.

☐ I want to live where the sun shines a lot.

☐ I want to live where I can grow my own food.

☐ I want to live wherever my friends live.

☐ I want to live where it is not too hot.

B Discuss your answers with a partner. Complete the Venn diagram below.

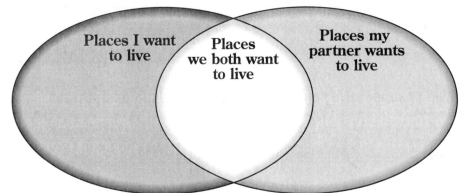

Places I want to live

Places we both want to live

Places my partner wants to live

C Study the chart.

Adverbial Clauses of Place		
Main clause	**Subordinate conjunction**	**Subordinate clause (dependent clause)**
I want to live	where, somewhere	I can go running in the morning.
I try to exercise	wherever	I can find a place.
He found a gym	everywhere	he went.
He didn't find a gym	anywhere	he went.
• Many times, the place clause can go first and is offset from the main clause by a comma.		
Wherever I find a place, I exercise. Everywhere he went, he found a gym.		Where he was, he was happy. Anywhere he lived, he was unsatisfied.
• Subordinate adverbial clauses have a subject and verb construction, but are dependent on the main clause for their meaning.		

D Look over the preferences from Exercise A again. Underline the adverbial time clause.

EXAMPLE: I want to live <u>where I can go running every day</u>.

1. She wants to live wherever the mountains are.

2. Anywhere they can see the ocean, they want to live.

3. I want to live anywhere there is no pollution.

4. Wherever the sun shines a lot, Kimla wants to live.

5. I want to live somewhere I can grow my own food.

6. Wherever my friends live, I want to live.

E Unscramble the words to write adverbial clauses.

EXAMPLE: the / wherever / is / air / clean _____ wherever the air is clean _____

1. the / wherever / is / and / organic / food / fresh

_____

2. a cool breeze / I / on / feel / where / my face / can

_____

3. safe / anywhere / is / thinks / she /

_____

4. there / wherever / is / light / a lot / of

_____

5. are / anywhere / the / offices / sanitary

_____

6. for / I / is / everywhere / go / adventure

_____

F Using the adverbial clauses you wrote above, write complete sentences.

EXAMPLE: <u>I like to play soccer wherever the air is clean.</u>

1. _____

2. _____

3. _____

4. _____

5. _____

6. _____

CHALLENGE 2 ➤ Adverbial Clauses of Time

A Read the conversation. Then, practice it with a partner.

Receptionist: Dr. Franklin's office.
Patient: My name is Orlando Colato. I have some questions about my bill.
Receptionist: Of course, Mr. Colato. Um, we have two Orlando Colato's. What is your birth date?
Patient: It is August 12, 1962.
Receptionist: Ok, I have your file right here. This shows that you owe $2000.
Patient: Yes, I know, but the bill is incorrect.
Receptionist: What seems to be wrong?
Patient: This bill says I had three examinations in March. The first was a physical for $280. Then, there is a second physical with an x-ray for $398. The third is for a procedure I am not familiar with.
Receptionist: Our records show you came in for each appointment, sir.
Patient: I did come in for a physical, but I didn't have an x-ray. That was my only appointment in March.
Receptionist: You know, I think we confused you with the other patient with your same name.
Patient: Yes, that makes sense. Can you please correct it?
Receptionist: Yes, of course. I will call you after I have entered the changes.
Patient: OK, as soon as you clear this up, I will be happy to pay my bill.
Receptionist: OK, thanks for calling and sorry for the inconvenience.

B Imagine that you are the receptionist. She needs to write a summary of the error. Write the summary on another piece of paper. Make sure you write the events in chronological order.

Adverbial Clauses of Time		
Main clause (independent clause)	**Subordinate conjunction**	**Subordinate clause (dependent clause)**
I spoke to you	after	you examined me on Friday.
Don't pay anything	before	you get an itemized bill.
She felt sicker	when	she saw the bill.
He made the co-pay	while	she was being examined.
We'll send your bill	as soon as	your insurance pays their portion.
She explained the situation	once	the patient calmed down.
• The time clause can also go first and is followed by a comma.		
After you called me on Friday, I spoke to you.		
While she was being examined, he made the co-pay.		
• Subordinate adverbial clauses have a subject and verb construction, but are dependent on the main clause for their meaning.		

C Circle the adverbial time clause in each statement.

EXAMPLE: (When she called her) name, Kate went in for her appointment.

1. He filled his prescription as soon as he left the doctor's office.

2. While her sister was waiting in the car, she quickly ran in to fill out the form.

3. I called the insurance company after I got the hospital bill.

4. The doctor finished the exam before his next patient arrived.

5. Once the insurance company fixed the mistake, we felt much better.

6. When the insurance representative called, we were out to lunch.

D Rewrite each main clause and subordinate clause into a complete statement by adding a subordinating conjunction.

EXAMPLE: I called the office. They sent me an itemized bill.
After I called the office, they sent me an itemized bill.

1. She got a call from the insurance company. She filled out the application.

2. The nurse explained the charges. He discussed the charges with his wife.

3. Liza called the doctor's office. They sent her a duplicate bill.

4. She recovered from surgery. She went back to work.

5. She called her family and friends. Dinuka received her diagnosis.

6. Brent got laid off from work. He starting looking for private insurance.

E Think about a recent experience you have had with a doctor, hospital, or insurance company. Write a brief summary of your experience using sentences with adverbial time clauses. Make some notes below about the order of events and then write your summary on a separate piece of paper.

1. _____   5. _____

2. _____   6. _____

3. _____   7. _____

4. _____   8. _____

Health

CHALLENGE 3 ➤ Adverbial Clauses of Reason

A Look at the chart about PPOs and HMOs.

PPO	HMO
Higher Co-pay	Low or sometimes free co-pay
Higher out-of-pocket expenses	Low or sometimes no out-of-pocket expenses
You can see any doctor you want to at any time.	You must choose one primary-care physician. You must get a referral from your primary-care physician to see another doctor.
Higher monthly premium	Lower monthly premium

B From the chart, it seems like HMOs are better. What is the advantage to having a PPO?

_____

C What is your preference? What is your partner's preference? Write sentences explaining why.

You: _____

_____

Your partner: _____

_____

Adverbial Clauses of Reason		
Main clause	**Subordinate conjunction**	**Subordinate clause (dependent clause)**
Health insurance is important	because	you never know when there might be an emergency.
The insurance paid the bill	since	we paid all the premiums on time.
The insurance questioned the charges	as	we had quite a few visits in one month.
You can get hip surgery	now that	you have health insurance.
He will keep the PPO	as long as	the premiums don't get too expensive.

• The reason clause can also go first and is followed by a comma.

Since we paid all the premiums on time, the insurance paid.
As long as the premiums don't get too expensive, we will keep the PPO.

• Subordinate adverbial clauses have a subject and verb construction, but are dependent on the main clause for their meaning. Adverbial clauses of reason tell why something happens or is done.

D Match a main clause to a subordinate clause to make complete sentences.

1. _e_ He can see any doctor he wants

2. ___ Owen and his brother need insurance

3. ___ They had to mail in their co-pay

4. ___ As long as she stays healthy

5. ___ My company will stay with the same insurance

6. ___ He thinks he doesn't need insurance

7. ___ It's hard to get insurance

8. ___ Now that all the surgeries are over

9. ___ Since she has a pre-existing condition

10. ___ Her bills were outrageous

a. since they forgot to pay it at the office.

b. as long as the employees are happy with it.

c. as he never gets sick.

d. since you smoke.

e. because he has a PPO.

f. she can't find insurance coverage.

g. since she doesn't have insurance.

h. she will begin physical therapy.

i. now that they have started a new business.

j. her premiums will be low.

E Complete each main clause with an adverbial clause of reason.

EXAMPLE: He will never use that company again because ____their fees were too high.____

1. Her bills are all paid now that _____.

2. He started exercising five days a week because _____.

3. The doctor said she could eat red meat again as long as _____.

4. Since _____, the insurance company denied the claim.

F Complete each adverbial clause of reason with a main clause.

EXAMPLE: ___He had to call the insurance company five times___ since they weren't returning his calls.

1. As long as you pay your co-pays, _____

2. _____ because he never eats fruits and vegetables.

3. _____ as they never paid the bill.

4. Now that she is well again, _____

G Answer each question about yourself.

EXAMPLE: Do you have health insurance? ___I have health insurance since my company pays for it.___

1. Do you eat healthy every day?

_____

2. Do you exercise?

_____

3. Do you go to the doctor for regular checkups?

_____

Health

CHALLENGE 4 ➤ Adverbial Clauses of Concession

A Write a sign of each addiction.

EXAMPLE: caffeine: <u>A person has to have a cup of coffee every morning or he or she gets a headache.</u>

1. gambling: _____

2. shopping: _____

3. internet: _____

4. TV: _____

5. nicotine: _____

6. food: _____

B Discuss your answers with a group. Do you agree or disagree?

C Study the chart.

Adverbial Clauses of Concession		
Main clause	**Subordinate conjunction**	**Subordinate clause (dependent clause)**
He says he doesn't have a gambling problem	although	he spends a lot of time in Vegas.
She tries to stop eating so much	though	she still eats over 4000 calories a day.
He smokes 3 packs of cigarettes a day	even though	he says he is quitting.
We are good students	in spite of the fact that	we are addicted to shopping.
The doctor said to take the medicine	even if	I don't like the taste.
* *though* is the same as *although* but less formal. *Even though* shows a stronger contrast.		
• The clause of concession can always go first and is offset from the main clause by a comma.		
Although he spends a lot of time in Vegas, he says he doesn't have a gambling problem. Even though he says he is quitting, he smokes 3 packs of cigarettes a day.		
• Subordinate adverbial clauses have a subject and verb construction, but are dependent on the main clause for their meaning. Adverbial clauses of concession show a contrast to the main clause.		

D Choose one main clause and one subordinate clause and write complete sentences.

Main	Subordinate
he says he is not obsessive compulsive	though she says she is not addicted to the Internet
she spends her days in front of the computer surfing the Web	even though he thinks he doesn't have a problem
~~she insists she does not have a sweet tooth~~	although she says she is not a shopaholic
she goes to the mall at least once a day	~~in spite of the fact that she eats a piece of chocolate after every meal~~
he exercises up to three times a day	though he washes his hands at least 20 times a day

EXAMPLE: She insists she does not have a sweet tooth in spite of the fact that she
eats a piece of chocolate after every meal.

1. _____

_____

2. _____

_____

3. _____

_____

4. _____

_____

E Look back at the ideas you wrote for Exercise A. Make statements using the conjunction given.

EXAMPLE: (even though) Even though she has to have a cup of coffee every morning
or she gets a headache, she says she is not addicted to caffeine.

1. (although) _____

_____

2. (in spite of the fact that) _____

_____

3. (though) _____

_____

4. (even though) _____

_____

5. (in spite of the fact that) _____

_____

Health

CHALLENGE 5 ➤ Adverbial Clauses of Purpose and Manner

A Match the questions with the correct answers.

Questions

__d__ 1. Why call a poison control center?

_____ 2. Why do you apply pressure to a wound that is bleeding?

_____ 3. Why do you cover someone who is shivering?

_____ 4. Why do you keep a wound clean?

_____ 5. Why do you give someone with chest pains an aspirin?

_____ 6. Why do you keep a person who has a head injury from sleeping?

Answers

a. to avoid infection

b. because he may have a concussion

c. because he or she may be in shock

d. because treatment for poison is different for different substances

e. to stop the bleeding

f. because he or she may be having a heart attack and it could save a life

B Study the chart.

Adverbial Clauses of Purpose and Manner		
Main clause	**Subordinate conjunction**	**Subordinate clause (dependent clause)**
You need to add pressure	so that	you can stop the bleeding.
Put the feet up	in order that	the blood goes to the heart and brain.
Keep medicines away from children	as	they could accidentally ingest it.
He is shivering	as if	he is in shock.
She looks	as though	she needs to lie down.

• Some clauses of purpose or manner can go first and are offset from the main clause by a comma.

As they can accidentally ingest it, keep medicines away from children.

• Subordinate adverbial clauses have a subject and verb construction, but are dependent on the main clause for their meaning. Adverbial clauses of purpose or manner describe the purpose of the action in the main clause.

C Complete each statement with an adverbial clause from the box.

> in order that he can get a second opinion
>
> as if she has a headache
>
> ~~in order that she can be there when her contractions get stronger~~
>
> as though she has never gotten a shot before
>
> as she will need her strength to make it though her physical therapy
>
> so that he can get his prescription filled
>
> needs to lie down and rest

EXAMPLE: Call her doctor <u>in order that she can be there when her contractions get stronger.</u>

1. He seems as though he _____.
2. She is holding her head _____.
3. He wants to call the pharmacist _____.
4. He should call another doctor _____.
5. She needs to rest _____.
6. She is talking _____.

D Take the questions and answers from Exercise A and make complete statements.

EXAMPLE: <u>You should call a poison control center because treatment for poison is different for different substances.</u>

1. _____
2. _____
3. _____
4. _____
5. _____

E Write sentences of advice for the following people.

EXAMPLE: My hand is bleeding. <u>You should clean it and cover it with a bandage so that it doesn't get infected.</u>

1. My head is hurting. _____
2. I feel dizzy. _____
3. He is choking. _____
4. She got burned. _____

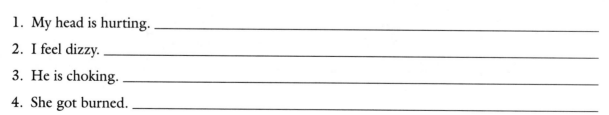

EXTENSION CHALLENGE 1 ➤ Adverbial Clauses of Condition 1

A Match the doctor's instructions with the ailment.

a. heart problems   b. obesity   c. heartburn   d. diabetes

___c___ 1. Please take this medicine three times a day before meals. It will help your digestion and you should be able to sleep through the night. Call me if you have problems. If you don't take the medicine, your problem will get worse.

_____ 2. You need to exercise. Dieting isn't enough. Exercise a minimum of 30 minutes a day and continue with the low-fat diet. You will lose weight provided that you diet and exercise.

_____ 3. Make sure you inject the insulin and check your blood sugar on a daily basis. You should keep a little candy close by just in case of emergency as well. Also make sure you eat at the same time every day.

_____ 4. If you feel chest pains, take an aspirin immediately and call me. If your left shoulder is bothering you, do the same. Call 911 if the pain gets severe.

B Study the chart.

Adverbial Clauses of Condition 1			
Main clause	**Subordinate conjunction**	**Subordinate clause (dependent clause)**	
The doctor will be unhappy	if	you don't take your medication.	
She will be on time for her appointment	unless	the bus is late.	has the opposite meaning of *if*
They will be on time for the appointment	provided that	the bus is on time.	has a similar meaning to *if*
He will get better	only if	he follows the doctor's instructions.	more definite than *if*

• The clause of condition can always go first and is offset from the main clause by a comma.

If you don't take your medicine, the doctor will not be happy.

• Subordinate adverbial clauses have a subject and verb construction, but are dependent on the main clause for their meaning. Adverbial clauses of condition show the circumstances when the main clause is true.

C Complete each statement with an appropriate subordinate conjunction. In many cases more than one conjunction will fit.

if	unless	provided that	only if

EXAMPLE: They will be less hungry _____ if _____ they eat balanced meals.

1. They can afford all of the out-of-pocket expenses _____ the insurance company decides not to fully cover the procedure.

2. That doctor said I would get better quickly _____ I eat right, exercise, and take my medicine.

3. He can't get to his appointments _____ someone drives him.

4. She can get the liver transplant _____ her body is strong enough to survive the surgery.

5. His diagnosis will stay the same _____ he continues to live his life in the same manner.

6. The doctor said I could go home _____ my blood pressure stays down.

D Help the doctor complete his checklist for patients by coming up with three ideas for each.

1. You will stay healthy .... provided that _____ you eat healthy and exercise. _____

 .... only if _____

 ... unless _____

2. You can leave the hospital .... provided that _____

 .... only if _____

 ... unless _____

3. You can eat junk food .... provided that _____

 .... only if _____

 ... unless _____

4. You can exercise .... provided that _____

 .... only if _____

 ... unless _____

E You know your body best. Write three "health-related" statements about yourself.

EXAMPLE: I can eat ice cream provided that I only eat it once a week. _____

1. _____

2. _____

3. _____

Adverbial Clauses of Condition 2

EXTENSION CHALLENGE 2 ➤ Adverbial Clauses of
Condition 2

A Read the paragraph and then list the preventative steps mentioned. Add any additional ones you can think of.

Preventative Medicine

Many Americans ignore their health or think that they are healthy when they are not. It is amazing how many people have had heart attacks in the United States because they didn't get an annual check-up and were unaware of their overall health. Some people think doctors are only for sick people. They forget that preventative steps to safeguard their health can save their lives and maybe extend it by many years. Doctors may prescribe simple medications for lowing blood pressure or cholesterol. They will most likely also suggest exercise and a good diet for their patients. It's important to listen to your doctor in order to protect yourself against common diseases.

 get an annual checkup _____   _____

_____   _____

_____   _____

_____

B Study the chart.

Adverbial Clauses of Condition 2		
Main clause	**Subordinate conjunction**	**Subordinate clause (dependent clause)**
You should take an aspirin a day	whether or not	you have any chest pains.
You should always be prepared	in case	there is an emergency.
You should get a second opinion	even if	you are satisfied with the first.
• The clause of condition can always go first and is offset from the main clause by a comma.		
Even if you are satisfied with the first opinion, you should get a second.		
• Subordinate adverbial clauses have a subject and verb construction, but are dependent on the main clause for their meaning. Adverbial clauses of condition show the circumstances when the main clause is true.		

C Match each main clause to a subordinate clause. Then, rewrite the sentences on the lines below.

1. __c__ She can take you to the doctor   a. in case there is an emergency.

2. _____ He could look for another doctor   b. even if she moves far away.

3. _____ She should have an extra bottle of pills   c. whether or not she has to work.

4. _____ She will never change doctors   d. in case his doctor goes out of town.

5. _____ He should get another opinion   e. even if he likes the first one.

6. _____ He will leave all of his numbers   f. in case she forgets them at home.

EXAMPLE: _She can take you to the doctor whether or not she has to work._

1. _____

2. _____

3. _____

4. _____

5. _____

D Complete each statement with an adverbial clause.

EXAMPLE: You should drink water every day _____ _even if you drink other beverages._

1. You should take vitamins even if _____.

2. You shouldn't smoke even if _____.

3. You should have a list of emergency numbers in case _____.

4. You should visit your doctor regularly whether or not _____.

E Complete each statement with a main clause.

EXAMPLE: _You should drink water every day_ whether or not you drink other beverages.

1. _____ in case you can't afford the surgery.

2. _____ whether or not you like his advice.

3. Even if you feel healthy, _____

4. In case you start feeling dizzy, _____

UNIT **6**

Retail

CHALLENGE 1 ➤ Adjective Clauses with Subject Pronouns

A Discuss what you might consider when choosing where to shop. Add any additional considerations.

☐ store location   ☐ product quality

☐ store hours   ☐ price

☐ parking   ☐ service after purchase

☐ employees (salespeople and managers)   ☐

☐   ☐

☐   ☐

B Discuss your answers to Exercise A with a group.

Adjective Clauses with Subject Pronouns		
	Adjective clause	**Clause construction**
Person *(who)*	She is the salesperson *who was in the store yesterday.* The salesperson *who was in the store yesterday* was excellent. (*Who* is the subject of the adjective clauses and modifies the preceding noun.)	**relative pronoun + verb** who + was
Thing *(that or which)*	They bought the patio furniture *that was on sale*. The furniture *which is on sale* is beautiful. (*That* and *which* are the subject of the adjective clauses and modify the preceding noun.)	that + was which + is

- Restrictive adjective clauses give essential information.
    They bought the patio furniture *that was on sale*. This means there was some furniture that wasn't on sale and the clause specifies only the furniture on sale.
- Nonrestrictive adjective clauses give extra unnecessary information. Use commas to offset the clause and use *which* not *that* for things.
    They bought the patio furniture, *which was on sale*. This means all the furniture was on sale and the information was not necessary to distinguish it from other furniture.

C Choose the correct relative pronoun to complete each sentence and bubble in the circle.

	who	that/which
EXAMPLE: The store _____ I like best is far from my house.	○	●
1. The manager _____ runs that store says he'll match the price.	○	○
2. That product didn't come with the warranty _____ I wanted.	○	○
3. The woman _____ convinced me to buy it was nice.	○	○
4. I couldn't find the salesman _____ was helping me.	○	○
5. He bought the item _____ was the most expensive.	○	○
6. The speakers _____ came with a warranty were $700.	○	○

D Complete each sentence with an appropriate adjective clause.

EXAMPLE: The bed _that was the most comfortable_ didn't come with a box spring.

1. The coupon _____ isn't good any more.

2. The manager _____ explained the warranty to us.

3. She wanted to buy the furniture _____.

4. They found a car _____.

5. The girl _____ said she would get the owner.

6. He read a book _____.

7. She researched the MP3 players _____.

8. The refrigerator _____ was way out of our price range.

E Take the checklist from Exercise A and write sentences about what is important to you in a shopping experience.

EXAMPLE: _The location of a store that I like to go to must be very close to my house._

1. _____

2. _____

3. _____

4. _____

5. _____

6. _____

UNIT **Retail**

CHALLENGE 2 ➤ Adjective Clauses with Object Pronouns

A Answer the questions.

1. Do you get catalogs in the mail? _____ If so, which ones? _____

2. Do you shop from catalogs? _____ Why or why not? _____
   _____

3. What are the benefits of shopping from a catalog? _____
   _____

4. What are the disadvantages? _____
   _____

5. Do you shop online? _____ Why or why not? _____
   _____

6. What are some things you can shop for online? _____
   _____

7. What are the advantages of shopping online? _____
   _____

8. What are the disadvantages? _____
   _____

B Share your answers with a partner. Do you agree or disagree?

Adjective Clauses with Object Pronouns		
	Adjective clause	**Clause construction**
Person *(whom)*	She is the salesperson *whom I saw yesterday*. The salesperson *whom she spoke to* was excellent. (*Whom* is the object of the adjective clauses and modifies the preceding noun.)	**relative pronoun + subject + verb** whom I saw whom she spoke to
Thing (*that* or *which*)	They bought the patio furniture *that they found online*. The furniture *which I saw on sale* was beautiful. (*That* and *which* are the objects of the adjective clauses and modify the preceding noun.)	that they found which I saw

- Reduced clauses: The relative pronoun can be deleted if it functions as an object.
  She is the salesperson *(whom)* I saw yesterday.
  They bought the patio furniture *(that)* they found online.
- Relative pronouns cannot be deleted if they follow prepositions.
  The salesperson *to whom* she spoke was excellent.

C Unscramble the adjective clauses.

EXAMPLE: she / that / found ____that she found____

1. called / he / whom _____
2. she / that / buy / going to / is _____
3. whom / like / you _____
4. will / contact / I / whom _____
5. which / like / they / never _____
6. she / in class/ whom / met _____

7. our friends / that / bought _____
8. he / sold / which / me _____
9. that / are / eat / you / going to

_____
10. commissioned / whom / we _____

D Choose one of the adjective clauses you wrote in Exercise C to complete each sentence below.

EXAMPLE: The toys ___that she found___ were in a catalog.

1. The person _____ is listed on the Web site.
2. She found the computer _____ in a catalog.
3. He sent me the watch _____
4. The students _____ buy all their clothes from catalogs.
5. The representative _____ helped him place his online order.
6. They bought the furniture _____ at an online auction.
7. We bought the fruit _____ at a farmers' market.
8. The artist _____ sells his work only in his gallery.
9. The car _____ retails for over $40,000.
10. The manager _____ is not working today.

E Complete each statement with an adjective clause of your own.

EXAMPLE: The stores ____that I like to shop in____ are expensive.

1. I have never met a salesperson _____.
2. Those shoes _____ are killing my feet.
3. The girl _____ told me everything would be half price next week.
4. We bought some furniture _____.

F Write two of your own sentences containing adjective clauses about a shopping experience.

1. _____
2. _____

Retail

CHALLENGE 3 ➤ Adjective Clauses Using *When, Where, or Why*

A Discuss the following with a small group.

1 When would you shop online vs. at a store?

2. When would you use coupons?

3. Why would you look for a product with a warranty?

4. Why would you buy something at a garage sale or swap meet?

5. What are the places where you like to shop for clothing? For groceries? For electronics?

Adjective Clauses Using *When, Where, or Why*				
	Adjective clause	**Clause construction**		
		relative adverb +	subject +	verb
Place	The store *where we bought the furniture* didn't offer a product guarantee.	where	we	bought
	We bought a new guitar at a store *where they don't offer service guarantees*.	where	they	don't offer
Time	We bought the computer on the day *when they were offering extended warranties*.	when	they	were offering
	She never thought she'd see the day *when you could buy things on the internet*.	when	you	could buy
Reason	The reason *why they didn't buy the printer* is it printed too slowly.	why	they	didn't buy
	Slow service is the reason *why we never shop at that store*.	why	we	never shop

All adjective clauses have three essential components: 1. They contain a subject and a verb; 2. They begin with either a relative pronoun, *who, whom, whose, that* or *which*; or a relative adverb, *where, when,* or *why*; and 3. They function as an adjective.

B Underline the adjective clause and circle the correct relative adverb in each statement.

EXAMPLE: Did you find a place (when / (where) / why) they sell reusable bags?

1. The places (when / where / why) she is looking for a desk are all closed on Mondays.

2. The reason (when / where / why) I never shop at the supermarket is the fish isn't as fresh.

3. They went to a store (when / where / why) the salespeople work on commission.

4. Can we find a time (when / where / why) the mall is quiet and not crowded?

5. We buy our produce at a farm (when / where / why) they only grow vegetables.

6. I went looking for an umbrella on a day (when / where / why) it was raining.

7. He gave me a good explanation (when / where / why) that television didn't come with a warranty.

8. Her sister bought a restaurant (when / where / why) they used to serve Mexican food.

C For each of the nouns given, write an adjective clause using *when, where,* or *why.*

EXAMPLE: a store where they serve snacks while you shop

1. a reason _____

2. a time _____

3. a park _____

4. an afternoon _____

5. a place _____

D Share your adjective clauses with a partner. Now take your partner's adjective clauses and use them to write complete sentences or questions.

EXAMPLE: Have you ever been to a store where they serve snacks while you shop?

1. _____

2. _____

3. _____

4. _____

5. _____

Retail

CHALLENGE 4 ➤ Reduction of Adjective Clause to Adjective Phrase

A Read the refund policy.

> **Refund Policy:** The purchase must be returned in saleable condition. It must be in the original package and undamaged. No refunds or returns are permitted on opened software.

All cash and all check purchases will be refunded with cash provided that the purchase was made at the same store where the refund is requested. All credit card purchases will be refunded with a credit to the credit card used for the purchase. Refunds will only be made with purchases that are less than 14 days old. Any item over 14 days from purchase may be returned for a store credit. A receipt is required with all refunds and returns. Exceptions to this policy are rare and can only be made by the store general manager.

B You are a salesclerk of a store with the above policy. Check (✓) what you would do.

1. Monica purchased the stereo system a week ago. She used it for a week and now has to move. Her new apartment doesn't have room for the system. She wants to return it for a refund.
    ☐ Refund   ☐ Store Credit   ☐ No Return or Refund   ☐ Ask the Manager

2. David purchased a new computer and used it for three days. It stopped working. He doesn't want to get it fixed through the warranty. He wants to return it and get his money back. He has the receipt but he threw out the original packaging.
    ☐ Refund   ☐ Store Credit   ☐ No Return or Refund   ☐ Ask the Manager

3. The guitar Jonathan purchased is new and hasn't been used at all. He purchased it as a gift for his girlfriend. She was disappointed and said she would prefer something different for her birthday. He purchased it 5 days ago. The store where he purchased it doesn't have anything but guitars.
    ☐ Refund   ☐ Store Credit   ☐ No Return or Refund   ☐ Ask the Manager

C Study the chart.

Rule	Adjective clause to adjective phrase
Relative pronouns can be deleted if they function as objects. They cannot be deleted if they follow a preposition.	The salesperson (*whom*) I spoke to gave me a discount. The book (*that*) she bought can't be returned. The manager to *whom* I spoke solved the problem.
Relative pronouns can be deleted along with the *be* verb in the progressive or passive forms.	The store (*that is*) selling that book offers free bookmarks. He bought furniture (*that was*) made in Italy.
Relative pronouns can be deleted along with the *be* verb if they come before a preposition.	She found a bed (*that was*) on sale. Jason bought the guitar (*that was*) in the window.

- A clause is a group of words that include a subject and a verb.
- A phrase is a group of words that does not include a subject and a verb.

D If the adjective clause can be reduced, cross out the unnecessary words.

EXAMPLE: The warranty ~~that is~~ offered by that store is the best one I have seen.

1. The computer that David purchased stopped working.

2. The salesperson whom he bought it from doesn't work there anymore.

3. Did you see the customer who was standing here a few minutes ago?

4. The stereo system that is playing right now is too big for Monica's new place.

5. The receipt that she has is too old.

6. I saw the patio furniture that was advertised in the paper.

7. Did they look for a house that was in their price range?

8. We never buy any product that doesn't come with a warranty.

9. The new store that opened near our house is having a grand opening sale.

10. The couch that you sold me has fallen apart.

E Complete each statement with the given adjective clause. Reduce the clauses if necessary.

EXAMPLE: The products _____ they sell _____ don't appeal to us. (that they sell)

1. Benny bought a boat _____. (that was on sale)

2. He found a deal _____. (that he couldn't pass up)

3. The salesperson _____ was very helpful. (whom he bought it from)

4. Shari is looking for a computer _____ a 3-year warranty. (that comes with)

5. She has searched every store _____. (that she could find)

6. Kenneth hopes to surprise his wife with the new washer and dryer

_____. (that she has been wanting)

7. He found a set _____. (that comes with a free vacuum cleaner)

8. Hopefully, he can buy the ones _____. (that are on sale)

F Write two pairs of sentences. In each pair, write one sentence with an adjective clause and the other with a reduced clause.

EXAMPLE: The store that I love is closing.   The store I love is closing.

1. _____

2. _____

Retail

CHALLENGE 5 ➤ Appositives

A Read the following announcements.

1. We, the English students at Jefferson Adult School, want to sell our old English textbooks for pennies on the dollar.

2. The used TVs in our restaurant, selling for very cheap, will be available this Saturday only.

3. Our plan, to sell our antique furniture tables and chairs at an auction next week, is coming together.

4. That warehouse, the one with the gray door, will open at 8 A.M. to the public.

B Look back at the announcements and underline the phrases between the commas. Is this information necessary to the meaning of the sentence? Why or why not? Discuss with a small group.

C Study the chart.

Appositives	
Our financial advisor, *the woman whom our friends recommended to us,* suggests we put away money every month for retirement.	noun phrase
The ad, *the one with all the great pictures,* shows how versatile the jacket can be.	
Our plan, *shopping wisely,* helps us save money on everything we buy.	gerund phrase
Her idea, *buying the most expensive car,* will surely affect our budget.	
My goal, *to save as much money as I can,* will help us buy a car.	infinitive phrase
His suggestion, *to read all of the ads,* will take us forever.	
Appositives are nouns or noun phrases that rename nouns that they follow. There are three different types of appositives.	

D Underline the appositive in each statement. After each statement, write the type of phrase: *noun*, a *gerund*, or an *infinitive*.

EXAMPLE: Her new book, <u>the one with the red cover</u>, is selling like hotcakes. _____noun_____

1. The TV ad, running every hour on the hour, will sell lots of tennis rackets. _____

2. My idea, to put ads in all the local papers, may cost more than I think it will. _____

3. His business, the website giving medical advice, isn't doing very well. _____

4. The used bike sale, happening every Wednesday, has drawn people from all over the state.

_____

5. Our house, the brown one with the tiled roof, has been for sale for almost five months.

_____

6. Jared's plan, to sell all of his furniture, is a great idea since he won't be moving back

for at least two years. _____

7. Her wedding gown, the jeweled one with the pink lace, is not the prettiest wedding dress

we have seen. _____

8. Her ad, the one with the artist's drawing, has been receiving a lot of attention. _____

9. The farmers' market, the one on State Street, only has farmers from local farms. _____

10. Her suggestion, to move all of the sale items into the window, was a great one. _____

E Write your own appositive phrases to complete each statement.

EXAMPLE: His idea of fun, _____buying plane tickets at an auction,_____ makes me nervous.
(gerund)

1. Her car, _____, sold for more than $15,000. (noun)

2. The idea, _____, is really confusing. (infinitive)

3. Our children's clothing store, _____, will soon be
offering shoes as well. (noun)

4. The stroller he is trying to sell, _____, is too old to get
much money. (noun)

5. Her plan, _____, will surely work. (infinitive)

6. The sale, _____, should bring in a lot of money. (gerund)

F Think of three things you own that you would like to sell. Write statements
using appositives.

EXAMPLE: <u>My MP3 player, the newest one on the market, is for sale on eBay.</u>

1. _____

2. _____

3. _____

Adjective Clauses with *Whose* (sidebar)

EXTENSION CHALLENGE 1 ➤ Adjective Clauses with *Whose*

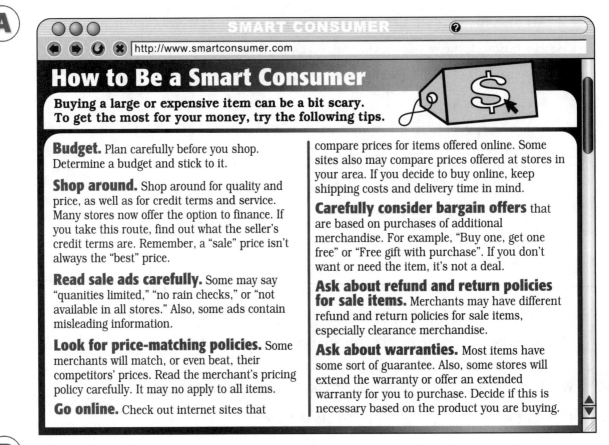

A

SMART CONSUMER

http://www.smartconsumer.com

How to Be a Smart Consumer

Buying a large or expensive item can be a bit scary.
To get the most for your money, try the following tips.

Budget. Plan carefully before you shop. Determine a budget and stick to it.

Shop around. Shop around for quality and price, as well as for credit terms and service. Many stores now offer the option to finance. If you take this route, find out what the seller's credit terms are. Remember, a "sale" price isn't always the "best" price.

Read sale ads carefully. Some may say "quanities limited," "no rain checks," or "not available in all stores." Also, some ads contain misleading information.

Look for price-matching policies. Some merchants will match, or even beat, their competitors' prices. Read the merchant's pricing policy carefully. It may no apply to all items.

Go online. Check out internet sites that compare prices for items offered online. Some sites also may compare prices offered at stores in your area. If you decide to buy online, keep shipping costs and delivery time in mind.

Carefully consider bargain offers that are based on purchases of additional merchandise. For example, "Buy one, get one free" or "Free gift with purchase". If you don't want or need the item, it's not a deal.

Ask about refund and return policies for sale items. Merchants may have different refund and return policies for sale items, especially clearance merchandise.

Ask about warranties. Most items have some sort of guarantee. Also, some stores will extend the warranty or offer an extended warranty for you to purchase. Decide if this is necessary based on the product you are buying.

B Rank the Web page suggestions 1-8. Write 1 next to the item you think is most important. Discuss your answers with a group.

C Study the chart.

Adjective Clauses with *Whose*	
Replacing a possessive adjective	**Clause construction**
I want to buy a cat. *Its* lineage should be purebred. Converts to: I want to buy a cat *whose* lineage is purebred.	*Whose* replaces a *possessive adjective* that precedes a person or a thing. It refers to both animate and inanimate nouns.
Robert bought a new TV. *His* old TV was broken. Converts to: Robert, *whose* old TV was broken, bought a new one.	
The family just moved in. *Their* house is for sale. Converts to: The family *whose* house is for sale just moved in.	*whose* + noun + verb

- The rule for restrictive and nonrestrictive clauses applies to these adjective clauses as well. When the clause is necessary for clarity, no commas are used to offset it.

D Take each sentence and separate it into two sentences.

EXAMPLE: They rented a barbecue whose grill was filthy.

<u>They rented a barbecue. Its grill was filthy.</u>

1. We don't know the person whose house we bought.

_____

2. A salesman, whose name I can't remember, told me it came with a warranty.

_____

3. I can't find the woman whose place in line I'm saving.

_____

4. Tina, whose computer is old, is looking for a new one.

_____

5. She found a clothing store whose clothes she couldn't live without.

_____

6. They live in a neighborhood whose houses are not selling.

_____

E Take each pair of sentences and combine them, using *whose*.

EXAMPLE: Henry bought a used motorcycle. Its chrome shined like new.

<u>Henry bought a used motorcycle whose chrome shined like new.</u>

1. We placed an ad for a new gardener. Our current gardener is moving.

_____

2. She met a store manager. She liked his personality.

_____

3. I found some new suitcases. I love the color.

_____

4. Erika walked into a store. The sale was in progress.

_____

5. We are trying to sell our boat. The engine needs some work.

_____

6. We came upon a restaurant. We love the food.

_____

UNIT

Retail

EXTENSION CHALLENGE 2 ➤ Adjective Clauses That Modify Indefinite Pronouns

A Read the conversation and practice acting it out with a partner.

Customer Service Representative (CSR): Can I help you?
Customer: Yes, I am very unhappy with this computer.
CSR: What seems to be the trouble?
Customer: Everything. It doesn't even start most of the time.
CSR: I am sure it can be fixed.
Customer: It is something that I don't want fixed. I want a new computer.
CSR: Well, I am not sure we can do that.
Customer: Why not?
CSR: The manufacturer will have to help you, I think.
Customer: That is not good enough. Is there someone in charge who can help me?
CSR: I will get the manager.
Customer: Thank you.

B Is the customer being reasonable? Discuss it with a group.

C Study the chart.

Adjective Clauses That Modify Indefinite Pronouns	
Person *(who)*	She is someone *who sells her fair share of cars*. Anybody *who shops like he does* must have a lot of money.
Thing *(that* or *which)*	Everything *(that) they bought* had to be returned. Anything *that glowed* she wanted to have.

• Indefinite pronouns are pronouns that are not specific like *someone* and *anything.* Indefinite pronouns include:

   another, anyone, anybody, anything, everyone, everybody, everything, nothing, each, either,
   no one, neither, nobody, one, someone, somebody, something, both, few, many, several

D **Circle the indefinite pronouns and underline the adjective clauses in the following sentences.**

EXAMPLE: She invited (everybody) that I like to the party.

1. Is there somebody that can do a price check for me?

2. He told me something that I will never forget.

3. They found many that they wanted to purchase.

4. After looking at both that she had bought, she decided she didn't like either of them.

5. Rusty can never find anything that he wants to wear.

6. The salesgirl brought me another that I could try on.

E **Write adjective clauses following the indefinite pronouns given.**

EXAMPLE: several _that she made_____

1. one _____

2. something _____

3. nothing _____

4. both _____

5. everyone _____

6. another _____

F **Share your adjective clauses with a partner. Take his or her clauses and write complete sentences.**

EXAMPLE: _When I saw her handmade aprons, I bought several that she made._____

1. _____

2. _____

3. _____

4. _____

5. _____

6. _____

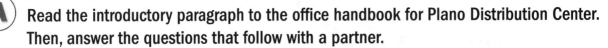
The Office

CHALLENGE 1 ➤ Nouns: Phrases, Pronouns, Clauses

A) Read the introductory paragraph to the office handbook for Plano Distribution Center. Then, answer the questions that follow with a partner.

    We would like to welcome you to the field services office of Plano Distribution Center. The office is the hub of our company. Your job is unique because we keep important and essential information in the office, items that cannot be replaced and which are confidential. You are required to use the fax machine, computer, shredders, and copy machines every day, and you are to avoid using any of this equipment for personal use. We are a company of integrity, so if our personal files on clients were to reach our competitors, it would be devastating to our company. You have signed a letter of agreement stipulating your willingness to work under these conditions. The company has invested millions of dollars into the equipment you will use. The following manual will give you an orientation identifying how to use much of it. You will also receive training, and we will provide technicians when necessary.

1. Why would your job be unique?

2. What are you required to do?

B) A noun is a person, place, or thing. Look back at the paragraph and underline every noun you can find. How many did you find?

C) Study the chart.

Nouns: Phrases, Pronouns, Clauses	
Definition	**Example sentences**
Pronouns: words that take the place of nouns including subject pronouns, object pronouns, possessive pronouns, and reflexive pronouns.	*It* is difficult. (subject) Javier loves *it*. (object) His computer is over there next to *mine*. (possessive) She sees *herself* in an office job in two years. (reflexive)
Noun phrase: a group of words with a noun as the main word.	*His job* is difficult. They need *three computers* for *the office*.
Noun clause: A group of words that have a subject and verb. The clause may function as a noun. It can be the subject or object of a sentence.	*What he does* is difficult. (subject) He loves *what he does*. (object)

D **Underline the noun phrases in the following sentences.**

EXAMPLE: <u>Your job</u> is unique because we keep <u>important and essential information</u> in <u>the office</u>.

1. We would like to welcome you to the field services offices of Plano Distribution Center.

2. The office is the hub of our company.

3. You have signed a letter of agreement stipulating your willingness to work under these conditions.

4. We are a company of integrity, so if our personal files on clients were to reach our competitors, it would be devastating to our company.

E **Circle the pronouns in the following sentences.**

EXAMPLE: (You) are required to use the fax machine.

1. We would like to welcome you to the field services offices of Plano Distribution Center.

2. The following manual will give you an orientation identifying how to use much of it.

3. Please make yourself familiar with it.

4. You will also receive training, and we will provide technicians when necessary.

F **Unscramble the noun clauses in each sentence.**

EXAMPLE: <u>What you see</u> is exactly what you will be doing. (you / what / see)

1. The trainer explained exactly _____. (I / supposed / what / to do / was)

2. _____ was the key to the supply closet. (found / what /she)

3. _____ was how to run the copy machine. (learned / what / she)

4. She figured out _____. (she / what / to do / likes)

G **Each sentence below is missing something, either a pronoun, a noun phrase, or a noun clause. Complete each sentence.**

EXAMPLE: She finished _____ the report. _____

1. Her boss told her _____.

2. _____ came and fixed the broken machine.

3. Could you help _____ figure this out?

4. I think I can do it by _____.

5. Did she ever learn how to operate _____?

6. _____ hope they will give _____ some time to study _____.

The Office

CHALLENGE 2 ➤ Noun Clauses as Objects of Prepositions

(A) Read the chart. Combine each problem and solution into a single sentence.

Problem	Solution
1. The secretary is concerned. The copy machine continually breaks down.	The manager asks the secretary to buy a new machine.
2. The secretary spoke to the manager. He sometimes treats the employees inappropriately.	The manager spoke with the secretary in private to understand her point of view and resolve the problem.
3. The secretary is interested in learning about new available software. She wants to hear what another employee has to say about it.	The manager set up a time for the employees to work together.
4. Several employees are on a committee to hire a new supervisor. They can't decide whom to hire.	The manager will make the decision.
5. The secretary went to the supply closet. The computer paper wasn't there.	The manager asks the secretary to complete a supply requisition.

1. <u>Because the secretary was concerned about the copy machine continually breaking down, the manager asked her to buy a new one.</u>

2. _____

3. _____

4. _____

5. _____

(B) Study the chart.

Noun Clauses as Objects of Prepositions		
	Preposition	Noun clause = object of the preposition
We are concerned	about	*what* she needs to do.
I am interested	in	*what* you have to say.
We can't decide	on	*who* we want for the new supervisor.
We went	to	*where* the paper was stored.
I spoke	about	*how* he treated other employees.

- A noun clause as the object of a preposition starts with a question word and is followed by a subject and verb.

Noun Clauses as Objects of Prepositions

C Choose an adjective clause to complete each sentence. More than one may fit.

... where the meeting was held   ... what she has to do next

... ~~what he learned~~   ... how to solve the problem

... who would make a good leader   ... what we can do to help

... who is giving the seminar   ... how we can work together

... where the conference is

EXAMPLE: She is interested in <u>what he learned.</u>_____

1. They are worried about _____

2. She came from _____

3. We will need to think about _____

4. She is concentrating on _____

5. He is interested in _____

6. I'm going _____

7. Our team needs to focus on _____

8. His speech was on _____

D Use one of the expressions from above to begin each sentence.

EXAMPLE: <u>We will need to think about</u>_____ how often we can meet.

1. _____ where the new office will be.

2. _____ when the shipment will arrive.

3. _____ where the money was last seen.

4. _____ how to repair the printer.

5. _____ what we can do to divide our time.

6. _____ what she can do for the company.

E Complete each statement about yourself with an adjective clause.

EXAMPLE: I'm excited about <u>who I will meet in class.</u>_____.

1. I came from a community _____.

2. I am interested in _____.

3. I like to think about _____.

4. I used to focus on _____.

5. I'm going to figure out _____.

6. I want to learn about _____.

UNIT 7 The Office

CHALLENGE 3 ➤ Noun Clauses as Complements

A Read the evaluation about Sarah.

Sarah is a good worker in the office. She is what I consider a model employee. I am particularly impressed by her organizational skills. She can find anything almost immediately. I am concerned that no one else may be able to understand her system, however. It seems that she works well in a team and people respect her, so hopefully she can teach others. She has complained in the past about how we do certain things. I feel what she has to say has merit.

B Answer the questions about the evaluation.

1. Would you say that this evaluation is mostly positive? Why or why not?

2. What is the problem with Sarah's organizational system?

3. Sometimes Sarah complains. Do you think her complaints will have a positive or negative outcome and why?

C A verb is an action or describes a state of being. Underline all the verbs that you can find in the evaluation above.

D Study the chart.

Noun Clauses as Complements			
Subject	Verb	Noun clause = Complement	Clause construction
It	seems	*that they work together well as a team.*	*that* + subject + verb
They	are	*what we would call well-organized.*	
She	became	*what they considered a problem in the office.*	
He	got	*what he wanted.*	*what* + subject + verb
You	felt	*what I said had merit, didn't you?*	
A complement always follows "to be", "to become", "to get", "to feel", or "to seem."			

E Look at the examples from Sarah's evaluation. Write a sentence that indicates the opposite idea.

EXAMPLE: She is what we would call well-organized.

<u>She is what we would call disorganized.</u>

1. She is what I consider a model employee.

_____

2. It seems that she works well in a team and people respect her.

_____

3. I feel what she has to say has merit.

_____

4. It seems that she can teach others.

_____

F Unscramble the noun clauses.

EXAMPLE: she / that / her / job / likes <u>that she likes her job</u>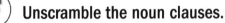

1. see / I / like / to / what _____

2. what / hoped / they / never / she / would _____

3. for / paid / what / he _____

4. *she / that / harder / could / work* _____

5. don't / to / like / very / they / hard / work / that _____

6. call / star / we / employee / a / what _____

G Choose a noun clause from Exercise F to complete each sentence.

EXAMPLE: It seems <u>that she likes her job.</u>

1. It seems _____.

2. She has become _____.

3. That is _____.

4. We all feel _____.

5. He is _____.

6. He got _____.

The Office

CHALLENGE 4 ➤ Noun Clauses as Subjects

Noun Clauses as Subjects

A Read the summary of the conflict resolution process.

How employees and management resolve conflicts at work can make a difference in employee satisfaction. All people involved should follow a set process. Where they start is the most important issue. First, set ground rules, show mutual respect, and be willing to listen to all sides. This is called setting the scene. Then everyone understands how each step makes the process work better. Follow this by gathering information about the problem. What is next seems simple. Identify and agree upon the problem. Once they do this, they can brainstorm how to resolve the problems. The final step will help everyone come to a mutual agreement. The solution should be beneficial to all parties, but especially to the company.

B Write each step of the process in Exercise A in order.

1. _____

2. _____

3. _____

4. _____

5. _____

C Study the chart.

Noun Clauses as Subjects		
Noun clause = Subject	Verb	
That our whole department got a raise	was	a surprise to us.
What we did yesterday	made	a big difference in office efficiency.
How she did her job	benefited	everyone.
Where I went	is	none of your business.
How they spoke to us	helped	me understand my job.

- A noun clause as a subject of the verb starts with a question word or *that* and is followed by a subject and verb.

D Underline the noun clauses as subjects. Then, circle the main verbs.

EXAMPLE: <u>Where you begin</u> (is) the most important part of conflict resolution.

1. How employees and management resolve conflicts at work can make a difference in employee satisfaction.

2. Where they start is the most important issue.

3. That everyone understands each other makes the process work better.

4. What is next seems simple.

5. What's important is identifying and agreeing upon the problem.

6. How you brainstorm can help you resolve the problem better.

7. That everyone comes to a mutual agreement is important.

8. What is important is that the solution is beneficial to all parties.

E Come up with a noun clause to begin each sentence.

EXAMPLE: <u>How you react</u> _____ can affect how the meeting will go.

1. _____ will help us make a final decision.

2. _____ seems really difficult.

3. _____ is coming up with a valid solution.

4. _____ will force us to work together.

5. _____ makes it easier to get along.

6. _____ benefited the whole team.

7. _____ seems like the hardest part.

8. _____ can force us to work harder.

F Imagine that you are creating a classroom conflict resolution manual. Write five statements to reflect your ideas.

EXAMPLE: <u>What is important is that we don't talk over one another.</u>

1. _____

2. _____

3. _____

4. _____

5. _____

UNIT **7**

The Office

CHALLENGE 5 ➤ Noun Clauses as Objects of Verbs

A Read the progress report outline.

Project: Keyless Entry Project

* how much of the work is complete

  _____

* what part of the work is currently in progress

  _____

* what work remains to be done

  _____

* what problems or unexpected things, if any, have arisen

  _____

* how the project is going in general

  _____

B Write the information below in the sections above.

* will complete a security scan of all employees, will train employees on keyless entry procedures and confidentiality

* re-keying the building and installing keyless entry system, starting a security scan of all employees, distributing key codes for keyless entry

* fair; contractor wants more money than he contracted for

* 80%

* employees have complained about some times when their current keys don't work

C Study the chart.

Noun Clauses as Objects of Verbs		
Subject + Verb	**Noun clause**	**Explanation**
I did	*what* I was asked.	• A noun clause as an object of the verb starts with a question word or *that* and is followed by a subject and verb. • In this case, the noun clauses are the object of the sentence.
She knows	*how* to do a PowerPoint presentation.	
They decided	*where* the location would be.	
My boss asked	*who* would be best for the job.	
I hope	*that* they worked as a team.	

D Answer each question with the noun clause given. Write complete sentences.

EXAMPLE: *Q:* What did you do?   *A:* (what she wanted me to)

I did what she wanted me to.

1. *Q:* What do they do?   *A:* (what they love)

_____

2. *Q:* What does she hope?   *A:* (that she will get some time off for all her hard work)

_____

3. *Q:* What did he ask?   *A:* (how to complete the application form)

_____

4. *Q:* What will we organize?   *A:* (what parts should go where)

_____

5. *Q:* What do you know?   *A:* (where the human resources office is)

_____

6. *Q:* What are they going to decide?   *A:* (how to divide the teams)

_____

7. *Q:* What did you decide?   *A:* (what office I would work best in)

_____

8. *Q:* What did she plan?   *A:* (who would lead each part of the presentation)

_____

E Take the topics listed in Exercise A and write complete sentences.

EXAMPLE: I told him how much of the work is complete.

1. _____
2. _____
3. _____
4. _____

F Write your own noun clauses to complete the sentences.

EXAMPLE: I plan where to keep everything in my house.

1. I decided _____.

2. I know _____.

3. I will find _____.

4. I am going to ask _____.

The Office

EXTENSION CHALLENGE 1 ➤ Indirect/Reported Speech

Indirect/Reported Speech

A Read the "To Do List".

		TO DO LIST		
Date: July 11				
Completed	**Priority 1-3**	**Action item**	**Directed by whom**	**Time promised**
☐	_____	Reorganize files	me	8:30 A.M.
☐	_____	Make copies for board meeting	supervisor	4:00 P.M.
☐	_____	Set appointments for new hires	supervisor	4:00 P.M.
☐	_____	Write letters for sales reps	sales reps	4:00 P.M.
☐	_____	Have fax machine fixed	office staff	12:00 P.M.
☐	_____	Have lunch with Bill	me	ongoing
☐	_____	Train new office staff	manager	ongoing
☐	_____	Answer customer phone calls	sales reps	4:00 P.M.
☐	_____	Complete call log	reps/superv	4:00 P.M.
☐	_____	Send thank you notes to staff	me	

B What do you think the priorities should be? Complete the priority column with your ideas and discuss them with a group.

C Study the chart.

Direct Speech	Indirect/Reported Speech
The manager told me, "Please *make* copies."	The supervisor told me *to make* copies.
Marco asked, "Who *will* be the best for the job?"	My boss asked who *would* be best for the job.
Nedia said, "I *want* to work in the mornings."	Nedia said (that) she *wanted* to work in the mornings.
The manager announced, "I *give* you all raises."	The manager promised (that) he *had given* us all raises.
Eva asked, "What is it you *are doing* in the office today?"	Eva asked me what I *was doing* in the office today.

- In reported speech, the verb tenses change to the past of the direct speech form. With commands (the imperative), use the infinitive form.
  - simple present ⟶ simple past
  - present continuous ⟶ past continuous
  - simple past ⟶ past perfect
  - modal *will* ⟶ modal *would*
- The subject pronouns often change.
- Quotation marks are not used and there is no comma after *said, asked, promised,* etc.

D Underline the indirect speech in each statement.

EXAMPLE: The supervisor told me <u>I should clock in the second I get here.</u>

1. The manager asked who wanted to work overtime.

2. My coworker promised he would help me finish the project.

3. The staff said they needed more training.

4. Her supervisor told her to take the bigger office.

5. She explained he never completes his work by himself.

E Change each quote to a reported speech statement.

EXAMPLE: "Fix my broken computer," he pleaded.

   He pleaded that I fix his broken computer.

1. She demanded, "Reorganize those files!"

   _____

2. My coworker said, "Eli is going to make copies for the board meeting."

   _____

3. Jenna replied, "I already set up all the appointments for new hires."

   _____

4. "Would you please write letters for our sales reps?" her supervisor requested.

   _____

5. She announced, "I had the fax machine fixed."

   _____

6. "Bill, would you like to have lunch with me?" I asked.

   _____

7. Napila said, "I want to help train the new office staff."

   _____

8. "I have finally answered all of the customer phone calls," Cindy declared.

   _____

9. "Could you complete the call log?" Stephanie asked.

   _____

10. "I need to send thank you notes to the staff," I told myself.

   _____

The Office

EXTENSION CHALLENGE 2 ➤ Noun Clauses Using *Whether* and *If*

 Read the conversation.

Employee: Excuse me sir, may I ask you a few questions?
Supervisor: Sure, please come in and sit down.
Employee: I understand that there will be budget cuts this year.
Supervisor: Yes, that's right, but we don't know yet if any jobs will be cut.
Employee: I really wanted to discuss if I am doing a good job and have to worry.
Supervisor: You are doing a great job, but I still can't say whether or not that matters.
    It is up to the owner of the company.
Employee: Thank you for being honest with me. Let me ask you one more question.
Supervisor: No problem.
Employee: I am curious whether or not it would be a good idea to look for another job
    and if you can give me a letter of recommendation or not.
Supervisor: Please wait another month. I hope I will have answers for you by then.
    We would hate to lose you.
Employee: Thank you sir. I will consider it.

B **Consider the employee's questions. Write what she wants to know below.**

_____

_____

_____

_____

C **Study the chart.**

Noun Clauses with *Whether* and *If*		
Expression	***whether/if***	**Clause**
I don't know	*if*	we will keep our jobs (or not).
I wanted to know	*whether*	(or not) we would work Monday.
We discussed	*if*	he would continue with the project (or not).

- Use *whether* or *if* for statements where there is doubt to something being true or false. Using *or not* is optional but falls in a different place depending on which word you use. Either word can be used.

- *Whether* and *if* statements are sometimes considered embedded questions. Consider the following:

Will we keep our jobs?	I don't know if we will keep our jobs.
Would we work tomorrow?	I wanted to know whether we will work Monday.
Would he continue?	We discussed if he would continue.

D Practice writing the noun clauses with different expressions. There are nine different combinations.

Expression	Noun Clause
I don't know	if I want to look for a new job
I'm not sure	whether or not I can complete the project on time
I need to think about	if I should ask for a raise

EXAMPLES

1. I don't know if I want to look for a new job.

2. I don't know whether or not I can complete the project on time.

3. _____

4. _____

5. _____

6. _____

7. _____

8. _____

9. _____

E Answer each question by completing the answer with a noun clause.

EXAMPLE: Will we move offices? I'm not sure whether or not we will move offices.

1. Can she train the staff? He doesn't know _____.

2. Do you want to work weekends? I need to think about _____.

3. Have they ever gotten a raise? She hopes _____.

4. Would they remember to lock up the building? I'm not sure _____.

5. Will she ever find a new job? He can't tell _____.

6. Are we going to talk to the boss? We haven't decided _____.

7. Are the custodians finished replacing the broken lights? I haven't heard _____.

8. Could you trade shifts with me? Let me ask my husband _____.

F Answer the questions using *if* or *whether*.

1. Can you meet after class?

   _____

2. Will you be taking this same class next semester?

   _____

3. Are you going to sell your book when this class is finished?

   _____

UNIT 8 Civic Responsibility

CHALLENGE 1 ➤ Articles: *A, An,* and *The*

(A) Read the paragraph above and answer the questions.

Many people consider being a citizen of the United States a privilege. Certainly, citizens have specific rights. An immigrant who wants to become a citizen must establish himself or herself in the United States, learn English, and follow all the laws of the land. Since the laws for citizenship for other countries may be different from those of the United States, some people can have dual citizenship, meaning they can be citizens of the United States and another country at the same time. When a person takes the steps necessary to become a citizen and when all requirements are met, he or she takes an oath stating a willingness to obey the laws and support the country. This person is then known as a naturalized citizen and has all the rights of someone born in the country.

1. What is a naturalized citizen?

2. What is dual citizenship?

3. What are some of the requirements necessary to become a citizen?

(B) Underline all the nouns in the paragraph.

(C) Study the chart.

Articles: *A, An,* and *The*		
Rules (article + noun)	**Example**	**What it means**
a or ***an*** Use *a* or *an* when the noun that follows represents one of a class of things or when the sentence is making a generalization. *An* is used when the noun that follows starts with a vowel sound.	*A citizen* has specific rights.	a citizen = any citizen or just citizens in general; sometimes the speaker means all citizens
the Use *the* when the listener and the speaker both have the same specific idea in mind represented by the noun.	*The citizen* we spoke about yesterday has his rights.	the citizen = a specific person who has already been identified
Note: Singular count nouns must be preceded by an article, *this/that*, or a possessive adjective.		

D Underline all the articles in the sentences below. Then, discuss with a partner why *a/an* or *the* was used.

1. Many people consider being a citizen of the United States a privilege.

2. An immigrant who wants to become a citizen must establish himself or herself in the United States, learn English, and follow all the laws of the land.

3. When a person takes the steps necessary to become a citizen and when all requirements are met, he or she takes an oath stating a willingness to obey the laws and support the country.

4. This person is then known as a naturalized citizen and has all the rights of someone born in the country.

E Fill in each blank with the appropriate article.

EXAMPLE: ___The___ green card I have been waiting for finally came in ___the___ mail.

1. Do you know anyone who is _____ citizen?

2. Salwa is _____ refugee from the Middle East. _____ country she comes from doesn't allow emigration.

3. Ella is 35 and her mother just became _____ permanent resident.

4. Marna just got _____ green card. _____ card came in the mail yesterday.

5. Have you taken _____ citizenship test?

6. _____ citizenship class they offer at my school starts at _____ beginning of _____ month.

F Write a paragraph about someone you know who has gone through the citizenship process.

_____

_____

_____

_____

_____

_____

_____

_____

G Go back and underline your articles. Did you use the right ones?

Civic Responsibility

CHALLENGE 2 ➤ Definite Articles *vs.* Nothing

A Read a summary of the *amendments* in the *Bill of Rights.*

1. Freedom of religion, speech, press, assembly, petition
2. Freedom to bear arms
3. No quartering of soldiers
4. Freedom from unreasonable searches and seizures
5. Freedom from unlawful imprisonment
6. Right of a speedy and public trial
7. Right of trial by jury
8. Freedom from unusual punishment
9. Other rights of the people
10. Powers reserved to the states

B Read the situations. Identify the amendment you think is involved.

1. John has been accused of a crime. He is innocent and insists that he have a trial immediately to prove his innocence. _____

2. John has a permit to own a gun and keeps it in his home for protection. _____

3. John disagrees with the judge in his case and writes a letter to the newspaper. They publish it. _____

C Study the chart.

Definite Articles *vs.* Nothing		
Rules (article + noun)	**Example**	**What it means**
the Use *the* when the listener and the speaker both have the same specific idea in mind represented by the noun.	***The*** *rights* that citizens have include the right to vote.	the rights = specific rights outlined in the U.S. Constitution
ø Use no article with plural nouns when making generalizations.	*Citizens* have specific rights.	citizens = any citizen or just citizens in general; sometimes the speaker means all citizens
ø Use no article with noncount nouns when making generalizations.	*Justice* is another word for *fairness* under the law.	justice and fairness = generalizations that cannot be counted
ø Use no article with proper names unless the article is part of the name (The United States of America.)	*Judge Harvey Spanner* declared his support for the new mayor.	Judge Harvey Spanner = the name of the judge
Note: Singular count nouns must be preceded by an article, *this/that*, or a possessive adjective.		

Definite Articles *vs.* Nothing

D Underline the nouns in the following sentences. Which ones have articles or a word modifying the noun? Why? Some don't have articles. Why not?

EXAMPLE: The <u>residents</u> of her <u>town</u> called several town hall <u>meetings</u>.

1. The laws that we follow were written by our founding fathers.

2. People want to change the immigration system.

3. Candidates always promise more than they can deliver.

4. Do you think fairness was involved in his decision?

5. Dr. Stevens presented his paper on global warming.

6. The classes that we took prepared us to pass the interview.

E Complete each statement with the noun given. If necessary, put *the* in front of the noun.

EXAMPLE: (citizens) _____The citizens_____ of California recalled their governor.

1. (lives) We hope to save _____ of our soldiers in combat.

2. (happiness) _____ is something you can't put a price on.

3. (refugees) _____ from Vietnam settled in communities together.

4. (problems) We have found _____ with the green card system.

5. (crimes) _____ committed in that town are far more than those committed in other nearby towns.

6. (documents) He sent _____ I had been waiting for.

7. (belongings) The Fifth Amendment guarantees that _____ are protected from search and seizure.

8. (soldiers) _____ are brave.

9. (justice) Do you think that _____ was served?

10. (Senator Lyons) _____ voted against the bill.

F Rewrite the statements in complete sentences. Start each with *The Bill of Rights guarantees* . . .

1. <u>The Bill of Rights guarantees the freedom of religion, speech, press, assembly,</u>
   <u>and petition.</u>

2. _____

3. _____

4. _____

5. _____

6. _____

7. _____

8. _____

9. _____

10. _____

Civic Responsibility

CHALLENGE 3 ➤ *The* and Demonstrative Determiners

A Read about the Hamilton Club.

The Hamilton Club was established in 1965. It is a service organization with 3,200 members worldwide. The club helps provide food to underprivileged families. This organization is proud of the efforts made over the past forty years. To become a member of Hamilton, you must:

1. be willing to contribute to underprivileged families,

2. attend monthly meetings, and

3. take leadership roles in the club.

B Underline the words that refer to the Hamilton Club in the reading.

C Study the charts.

Rules	Examples	
Repetition: referents can be repeated as originally stated or parts of it can be repeated.	*The Hamilton Club* is a service organization. It has a long history. *The Club* was established in 1965.	*The Hamilton Club* is repeated in a shortened form *(The Club).*
Synonym: referent can be repeated as another word.	*The organization* is a service organization. *The group* was established in 1965.	*The group* is a synonym for the referent, which is *the organization.*
Classifier: A demonstrative determiner followed by a noun that classifies the referent is called a classifier.	*The Hamilton Club* is very interested in service. *This organization was* established in 1965.	*The Hamilton Club* has been classified as an organization here.
Paraphrase: The referent can be a process. When this is the case, the process can be given a new name usually preceded by *this.*	To join the Hamilton Club, you must be recommended by a member and then go through a ceremony. *This initiation* is a simple process.	*This initiation* refers to the process of becoming a member of the Hamilton Club.

Definitions	Example	
referent = a familiar word that is referred to later in a passage.	The Hamilton Club is a service organization. *It* was established in 1965.	*It* refers back to the referent, which is *the Hamilton Club.*
demonstrative determiners = *this, that, these, those.* Determiners combine with nouns.	Hamilton International is a service organization. *This organization* has over 3,200 clubs throughout the world.	*This organization* refers to *Hamilton International.*

D Underline the referents in the following statements.

EXAMPLE: <u>The Club</u> was established in 1989.

1. <u>The purpose of the organization</u> is to promote self-confidence and service.

2. <u>It</u> meets twice a month.

3. <u>This organization</u> only allows boys age 11 and older to join.

4. All members of <u>the group</u> must pay $45 annually.

E Complete the paragraph about The Mother's Club with phrases and words from the box. Use a different phrase in each blank.

~~The Mother's Club~~	the Club	the organization
the group	the Mother's Club	the Club's

_____The Mother's Club_____ (1) is a group of 35 dynamic women working

to help Northville school children excel by providing enrichment opportunities.

In 1935, _____ (2) of 12 women decided to meet

regularly for enlightenment and social activities. During the Depression of the 1930s,

_____ (3) held a fundraiser to purchase milk for school children

to drink with their lunches. _____ (4) fundraising has now grown

to three events each year, enabling them to donate approximately $30,000 annually to student

enrichment programs and activities. _____ (5) performs service

projects at the public school buildings on a rotating cycle, working at two or three schools each

year. As far as social events, _____ (6) has Book Club meetings

once a month and lunch and movie afternoons twice a year.

F Complete the following paragraph with your own referent phrases.

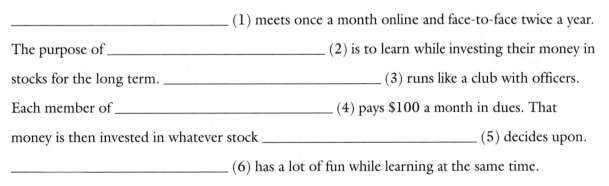

Five years ago, a group of friends who wanted to learn more about the stock market

got together and started an investment club. They call themselves the Bond Boys.

_____ (1) meets once a month online and face-to-face twice a year.

The purpose of _____ (2) is to learn while investing their money in

stocks for the long term. _____ (3) runs like a club with officers.

Each member of _____ (4) pays $100 a month in dues. That

money is then invested in whatever stock _____ (5) decides upon.

_____ (6) has a lot of fun while learning at the same time.

Civic Responsibility

CHALLENGE 4 ➤ Demonstrative Determiners and Pronouns

A Look at the suggestions about creating less trash. All are beneficial but some are easier than others. Check (✓) the five items you think are easiest to do.

Create Less Trash

☐ Buy items in bulk from loose bins when possible to reduce the packaging wasted.

☐ Avoid products with several layers of packaging when only one is sufficient.

☐ Buy products that you can reuse.

☐ Maintain and repair durable products instead of buying new ones.

☐ Check reports for products that are easily repaired and have low breakdown rates.

☐ Reuse items like bags and containers when possible.

☐ Use cloth napkins instead of paper ones.

☐ Use reusable plates and utensils instead of disposable ones.

☐ Use reusable containers to store food instead of aluminum foil and cling wrap.

☐ Shop with a canvas bag instead of using paper and plastic bags.

☐ Buy rechargeable batteries for devices used frequently.

☐ Reuse packaging cartons and shipping materials. Old newspapers make great packaging material.

☐ Buy used furniture. It is much cheaper than new furniture.

B Study the chart.

Demonstrative Determiners and Pronouns		
	Singular	Plural
Near	*this*	*these*
Far	*that*	*those*

Demonstratives determiners (or *adjectives*) tell the reader if the noun is near or far and singular or plural. *Demonstrative pronouns* represent a noun that is near or far and singular or plural. Nouns can be omitted if referred to previously.

	Examples	
Near (space)	*This* (trash can) is used for recycling.	The trash can is near the speaker.
Far (space)	*That* (trash can) is used for recycling.	The trash can is not within reaching distance of the speaker.
Near (time)	*These* (recycling systems) we learned about are great.	They learned about the recycling system a short time ago, probably the same day.
Far (time)	*Those* (recycling systems) we learned about are great.	They learned about the recycling system previously.

C Underline the demonstratives in each statement. Then, decide if the demonstratives are indicating near or far. Write *near* or *far* on the line.

EXAMPLE: <u>These</u> bottles are recyclable. _____near_____

1. That packaging can be reused. _____

2. Those napkins are cloth so we should use them. _____

3. Can these batteries be recharged? _____

4. Those suggestions we learned for creating less trash are really useful. _____

5. This maintenance plan is difficult to understand. _____

6. Those products in bulk from the market are a great deal! _____

7. This furniture is used, and it was so much cheaper than the new stuff we looked at. _____

8. Where did you get these reusable bags? _____

9. Why does the box need all those layers of packaging? _____

10. Did you see that report on those new products? _____   _____

D Complete each statement with *this, that, these,* or *those* based on the information given.

EXAMPLE: _____Those_____ washers are very efficient and use a very little amount of energy. (far)

1. _____ dryer costs you less money to operate because it is gas. (near)

2. How long have you had _____ water heater? (near)

3. Please don't open _____ oven door while the chicken is cooking. (far)

4. Did you wash _____ clothes with hot water or cold? (near)

5. She put _____ insulated blanket around her water heater. (near)

6. Do you know what temperature _____ refrigerator is set at? (near)

7. I replaced _____ filter on our air conditioning unit. (far)

8. We always unplug _____ appliances before we go away on vacation. (near)

9. _____ lint filter in our dryer is always full of lint. (far)

10. He always leaves _____ lights on, which drives me crazy! (far)

E Write four statements about things you do that are good for the environment. Try to use demonstratives.

1. _____

2. _____

3. _____

4. _____

UNIT Civic Responsibility

CHALLENGE 5 ➤ *Such* and Demonstrative Determiners

A Read one person's opinion of advantages and disadvantages of carpooling. Discuss it with a group. Which is better for you and why?

Advantages of Carpooling	Disadvantages of Carpooling
Expense: Share the expenses (car maintenance and gas) with others who drive. Your insurance will be cheaper too.	**Expense:** Family emergencies, outside appointments, or unexpected overtime may require making other, often costly, arrangements.
Stress: In busy areas driving can be very stressful. Sharing the driving responsibilities can reduce stress.	**Stress:** Sometimes those you are commuting with have bad habits, talk too much, don't talk enough, or complain about your driving.
Pollution and Congestion: Fewer cars because of carpoolers mean less pollution caused by motor vehicles.	**Pollution and Congestion:** In places with few cars and where commute time is very short, the advantages don't outweigh the disadvantages.
Convenience: People who work together and have the same work schedule can carpool. If the boss wants you to finish a project before you leave, you have a good excuse to leave it for tomorrow.	**Convenience:** Many people have varied work schedules that change regularly, they like to do errands on the way home or to work, and their car is available in case of emergency.
Time: The carpool or HOV (high occupancy vehicle) lane allows you to travel faster.	**Time:** Your starting and returning time is restricted by the people you carpool with.

B Study the chart.

Such and Demonstrative Determiners		
Determiner	**Example**	**Explanation**
this + noun Use *this* with singular nouns that represent specific things.	Her opinion is that we should all carpool. Is *this* opinion really based on reality?	*This* refers to the specific opinion that everyone should carpool.
such a(n) + noun Use *such a* with singular nouns that represent classes or subgroups of the nouns.	Her opinion is that we should all carpool. Is *such an* opinion really based on reality?	*Such an* is referring to any opinion like the one mentioned and not only the opinion that everyone should carpool.
these + noun Use *these* with plural nouns that represent specific things.	Carpool lanes with walls on either side can be dangerous in accidents. *These* lanes are difficult to merge in and out of.	*These* lanes refers only to the specific carpool lanes with walls on either side.
such + noun Use *such* with plural nouns that represent classes or groups that have been specified.	Carpool lanes with walls on either side can be dangerous in accidents. *Such* lanes are also difficult to merge in and out of.	*Such* lanes refers to all of those carpool lanes with walls on either side.
Use *this* or *such* with noncount nouns. Use *this* for specific and *such* for general.		

C Complete all of the A statements with *this* or *these* and all of the B statements with *such a/an* or *such*.

EXAMPLE: She thinks it is ridiculous to drive an SUV.

A. ___This___ idea isn't fair to all those parents who need larger cars for their families.

B. _Such an_ idea discriminates against parents who need larger cars for their families.

1. They stopped driving completely to save money on gas.

A. Is _____ situation really true?

B. Is _____ situation possible in a suburban neighborhood?

2. Some car companies are making more hybrid vehicles.

A. _____ vehicles are more expensive than the non-hybrid versions.

B. _____ vehicles could help save the environment.

3. Many gas stations are offering gas incentives.

A. Will _____ incentives really work?

B. Will _____ incentives really work?

4. People at my work have started carpooling.

A. _____ situation is happening more and more around the country.

B. _____ situations are happening more and more around the country.

D With a partner, discuss the difference in meaning between the A and B statements.

E Respond to each statement with your own opinion. Your opinion can be specific or general.

EXAMPLE: One company is trying to bring back the electric car.
Such innovations will surely help our environment.

1. Carpooling is a waste of time.

_____

2. You should try to walk instead of driving your car.

_____

3. Public transportation is a great way to get around.

_____

4. It is impossible for parents of small children not to be driving all over the place.

_____

5. Smaller cars are just as bad for the environment as bigger ones.

_____

Civic Responsibility

EXTENSION CHALLENGE 1 ➤ Review: Specific and General Determiners

A It is important to protect our natural resources. Work with a small group to come up with a list of ways to conserve water. Discuss which of your ideas will have the most impact on the environment.

1. _____
2. _____
3. _____
4. _____
5. _____
6. _____

B Study the chart.

Review: Specific and General Determiners		
	Singular	**Plural**
General	a right (indicates any right among others)	some rights (indicates more than one right among others, but not specific to which ones)
	Ø information (noncount–not singular or plural) (indicates information in general- not specific)	Ø (count nouns with no article indicates general categories and are not specific)
	such a right (indicates any member of rights)	such rights (indicates all rights within a class of rights)
	such information (noncount–not singular or plural) (indicates any information in a class)	
Specific	the right (indicates a specific right mentioned earlier)	the rights (indicates specific rights mentioned earlier)
	this right (indicates a specific right mentioned in the recent past)	these rights (indicates specific rights mentioned in the recent past)
	that right (indicates a specific right mentioned in the not-so-recent past)	those rights (indicates specific rights mentioned in the not-so-recent past)

C Complete the paragraph with an appropriate article or demonstrative. If no word is necessary, write ∅.

Our Most Precious Resource

Protecting (1) ____the____ environment we live in is (2) _____ duty. There

are many ways we can protect (3) _____ place we live, but I think one of

(4) _____ most important things we can do is conserve (5) _____ water.

(6) _____ idea is becoming very popular today. Why? Water is one of our most precious

resources. First of all, (7) _____ human body is made up of 75 percent water. We

could only live for one week without (8) _____ water; therefore we need to drink

(9) _____ water to survive. Another reason that water is so important is that we need it

to clean. We need water to clean (10) _____ bodies, wash (11) _____ dishes,

and launder (12) _____ clothes. Can you imagine not being able to do any of

(13) _____ things? Still another reason is that (14) _____ plants and trees

need (15) _____ water to grow and survive. Without (16) _____ plants and

(17) _____ tress, humans wouldn't survive because (18) _____ plants give off

(19)_____ oxygen that we need in order to breathe. For (20) _____ reasons, I

believe that we need to conserve our most precious resource-(21)_____ water.

Conserving water is simple. Take (22) _____ shorter showers. Put more clothes

in (23) _____ load of wash. Fill up (24) _____ dishwasher before you run it.

Turn off (25) _____ water while you are brushing your teeth. Water your plants less

often. Don't use (26) _____ hose to clean your patio and yard. Simple, right? Following

(27) _____ ideas could make (28) _____ big difference. So please, do your

part in trying to help save our planet.

UNIT **8**

Civic Responsibility

EXTENSION CHALLENGE 2 ➤ **Review: Demonstrative Forms, Pronouns, and Definite Articles**

A Look back at the *Bill of Rights* from Challenge 2. Which ones do you think are the most important? List them below in order of importance to you.

1. _____
2. _____
3. _____
4. _____
5. _____
6. _____
7. _____
8. _____
9. _____
10. _____

B Share your ideas with a partner. Do you agree or disagree with one another?

Review: Demonstrative Forms, Pronouns, and Definite Articles		
	Emphasis on the referent	**More emphasis on the referent**
The freedoms of religion, speech, press, and assembly are basic rights afforded to all Americans.		
They are part of the first amendments to the U.S. Constitution.	*The rights* are part of the first amendments to the U.S. Constitution.	*These rights* are part of the first amendments to the U.S. Constitution.
All citizens of the United States have the right to say what they believe within certain limits. The limits are often interpreted by the courts.		
Everyone should be aware of *them*.	Everyone should be aware of *the limits*.	Everyone should be aware of *these limits*.
The United States provides the opportunity to worship as we please.		
I really appreciate *it*.		I really appreciate *this (that)*.

C Complete each set of statements with words showing less emphasis to showing more emphasis. Follow the example.

EXAMPLE: Freedom of speech is a basic right. __*It*__ gives people the right to speak freely.

_____*The right*_____ of free speech is an important part of our constitution.

_____*This right*_____ has limitations.

1. There are certain limitations to the freedom of speech. _____ can be found in the Constitution. _____ come from the court's interpretations of the law. Some of _____ are often challenged.

2. Citizens do not have the right, for example, to incite or provoke violence. If _____ do this with words or actions, _____ can be arrested. _____ are disobeying a constitutional amendment.

3. Also, people cannot tell lies to ruin someone's reputation. Courts have ruled against _____ who do this in many cases. _____ are also accused of going against the first amendment.

4. Finally, this freedom does not include acts or words of obscenity. _____ one is more difficult since the concept of what is obscene is continually changing.

D Write a paragraph on what the freedom of speech means to you. Try to include demonstrative forms and pronouns.

_____

_____

_____

_____

_____

_____

_____

APPENDIX

➤ GLOSSARY OF GRAMMAR TERMS

adjective	a word that describes a noun (Example: The <u>red</u> hat)
adverb	a word that modifies a verb, adjective, or another adverb (Example: She <u>eats quickly</u>.)
affirmative	not negative and not a question (Example: *I like him.*)
animate/inanimate	objects that have action or motion (Example: <u>teacher</u> or <u>water</u>) / objects that don't have action or motion (Example: <u>book</u> or <u>desk</u>)
apostrophe	a punctuation mark that shows missing letters in contractions or possession (Example: *It<u>'</u>s* or *Jim<u>'</u>s*)
article	words used before a noun (Example: <u>a</u>, <u>an</u>, <u>the</u>)
base form	the main form of the verb, used without to (Example: <u>be, have, study</u>)
causative	a verb form that indicates that the subject of the sentence causes the object to do something. (Example: *I <u>made</u> her study.*)
clause	a group of words that has a subject and a verb. (Example: *We live here.*)
comma	the punctuation mark (,) used to indicate a pause or separation (Example: I live in an apartment, and you live in a house.)
comparative	a form of an adjective, adverb, or noun that expresses the difference between two or more things (Example: *My sister is <u>taller</u> than you.*)
complement	a word or words that add to or complete an idea after the verb (Example: He *is <u>happy</u>.*)
conditional, contrary-to-fact	a structure used for talking about an imaginary situation that is not true at the present time (Example: <u>If I won</u> the lottery, <u>I would buy</u> a mansion.)
conditional, future	a structure used for talking about possibilities in the future (Example: <u>If it rains, I will bring</u> an umbrella.)
conjugation	the forms of a verb (Example: *I <u>am,</u> You <u>are,</u> We <u>are,</u> They <u>are,</u> He <u>is,</u> She <u>is,</u> It <u>is</u>*)
conjunction	a type of word that joins other words or phrases (Example: Maria <u>and</u> Gilberto)
consonant	any letter of the alphabet that is not a vowel (Example: *b, c, d, f...*)
continuous form	a verb form that expresses action during time (Example: *He <u>is shopping</u>.*)
contraction	shortening of a word, syllable, or word group by omission of a sound or letter (Example: It is = <u>It's,</u> does not = <u>doesn't</u>)
count nouns	nouns that can be counted by number (Example: one <u>apple,</u> two <u>apples</u>)
definite article	use of *the* when a noun is known to speaker and listener (Example: I know <u>the</u> store.)
direct speech	a quotation of a speaker's exact words (Example: He said, <u>"I am sick."</u>)
embedded question	a question placed within another question or a statement (Example: *Do you know <u>when the bank opens?</u>*)

exclamation mark	a punctuation symbol marking surprise or emotion (Example: Hello!)
formal	polite or respectful language (Example: _Could_ you _please_ give me that?)
future tense	a verb form in the future tense (Example: I _will study_ at that school next year.)
gerund	an -ing form of a verb that functions as a noun (Example: _Swimming_ is fun.)
imperative	a command form of a verb (Example: _Listen!_ or _Look out!_)
implied condition	a kind of conditional sentence in which the if-clause is implied rather than stated (Example: _I would lend_ you money.)
indefinite article	_a_ or _an_ used before a noun when something is talking about for the first time or when _the_ is too specific (Example: There's _a_ new _restaurant_ in town.)
indirect speech	a form of a sentence that reports on what was said or written by another person (Example: _He said he was sick._)
infinitive	the main form of a verb, usually used with _to_ (Example: I like _to run_ fast.)
informal	friendly or casual language (Example: _Can I have that?_)
irregular verb	a verb different from regular form verbs (Example: be = _am, are, is, was, were, being_)
modal auxiliary	a verb that indicate a mood (ability, possibility, etc.) and is followed by the base form of another verb (Example: I _can_ read English well.)
modifier	a word or phrase that describes another (Example: a _good_ friend)
negative	the opposite of affirmative (Example: She _does_ _not_ like meat.)
noncount nouns	nouns impossible or difficult to count (Example: _water, love, rice, fire_)
noun	a name of a person, place, or thing (Example: _Joe, England, bottle_)
object, direct	the focus of a verb's action (Example: I eat _oranges_.)
object pronoun	replaces the noun taking the action (Example: _Julia_ is nice. I _like her_.)
passive voice	a sentence structure in which the subject of the sentence receives rather than performs the action (Example: _The window was opened_.)
past continuous	a verb form that expresses an action in progress at a specific time in the past (Example: I _was reading_ a book at 8:00 last night.)
past perfect	a verb form used to express an action or a state in the past that happened before another action or state in the past (Example: I _had_ already _eaten_ when he invited me out to dinner.)
past tense	a verb form used to express an action or a state in the past (Example: You _worked_ yesterday.)
period	a punctuation mark of a dot ending a sentence (.)
phrasal verb	a verb consisting of a verb plus an adverb or preposition(s), that has a meaning different from the words it is made up of (Example: _call up, write down, run out of_)
plural	indicating more than one (Example: _pencils, children_)

possessive adjective	an adjective expressing possession (Example: <u>our</u> cat)
possessive pronoun	a word which takes the place of a noun and expresses ownership (Example: The *hat* is <u>mine</u>.)
preposition	a word that indicates relationship between objects (Example: The *pen* is <u>on</u> the *desk*.)
present perfect	a verb form that expresses a connection between the past and the present and that indicates indefinite past time, or continuing past time (Examples: I <u>have lived</u> in Paris. She <u>has worked</u> here for three years.)
present perfect continuous	a verb form that focuses on the duration of an action that began in the past and continues to the present. (Example: I <u>have been waiting</u> in line for an hour.)
present tense	a verb tense representing the current time, not past or future (Example: *They* <u>are</u> *at home right now.*)
pronoun	a word used in place of a noun (Example: *Ted is 65.* <u>He</u> *is retired.*)
question form	a structure that asks for an answer (Example: <u>Where is my book?</u>)
regular verb	verb with endings that are regular and follow the rule (Example: work = *work, works, worked, working*)
reporting verb	a verb used to express what has been said or written (Example: She <u>said</u> that she was leaving. He <u>complained</u> that he was cold.)
sentence	a thought expressed in words, with a subject and verb (Example: <u>Julia works hard.</u>)
short answer	a response to a *yes/no* question, usually a subject pronoun and auxiliary verb (Example: <u>Yes, I am.</u> <u>No he doesn't.</u>)
singular	one object (Example: <u>a cat</u>)
statement	a sentence (Example: <u>The weather is rainy today.</u>)
subject	the noun that does the action in a sentence (Example: <u>The</u> <u>gardener</u> *works* here.)
subject pronoun	a pronoun that takes the place of a subject (Example: *John* is a student. <u>He</u> is smart.)
superlative	a form of an adjective, adverb, or noun that expresses the highest quality or degree of something (Example: <u>tallest</u>, <u>happiest</u>, <u>most comfortable</u>, <u>most beautiful</u>)
syllable	a part of a word as determined by vowel sounds and rhythm (Example: ta-*ble*)
tag question	a short informal question that comes at the end of a sentence in speech (Example: *You like soup,* <u>don't you?</u> *They aren't hungry,* <u>are they?</u>)
tense	the part of a verb that shows the past, present, or future time (Example: He *t*al<u>ked</u>.)
verb	word describing an action or state (Example: The boys <u>walk</u> to school. I <u>am</u> tired.)
vowels	the letters *a, e, i, o, u,* and sometimes *y*
wh- question	a question that asks for information, usually starting with *Who, What, When, Where,* or *Why.* (Example: <u>Where</u> do you live?) *How* is often included in this group.
yes/no question	a question that asks for an affirmative or a negative answer (Example: <u>Are you</u> <u>happy?</u>)

➤ GRAMMAR REFERENCE

Gerunds as Objects of Prepositions			
Verb	Preposition	Gerund	Example sentence
learn learn best	by	writing participating	He **learns by writing** everything down. They **learn best by participating** in a discussion.
learn	through by	repeating watching	They **learn through listening**.
practice	by	relating solving	We **practice by repeating** what we hear. I **practice by watching** a video.
(be) good	at	remembering	Logical learners **are good at solving** problems.
excel	in	taking	You **excel in remembering** information.
succeed	in	listening	I **succeed in taking** good notes.
struggle	with	identifying	That student **struggles with listening** in class.

Gerunds as Direct Objects			
Verb	Infinitive or Gerund	Example sentence	Other verbs that follow the same rule
want plan	+ infinitive	He **wants to study** art. He **planned to learn** English.	arrange, choose, decide, expect, hope, prepare, resolve
enjoy finish	+ gerund	She **enjoys fixing** cars. She **finished studying** for the test.	anticipate, consider, complete, discuss, imagine, necessitate, recommend
like	+ infinitive or + gerund	They **like to paint**. We **like painting**.	begin, commence, continue, love, prefer, try

infinitive = *to* + verb

gerund = verb + *ing*

Simple Past/Present Perfect/Simple Present		
Simple Past	Something that started and ended in the past.	Juan was born in 1989.
Present Perfect	Something that started in the past and continues in the present.	Juan has been in the United States for three years.
Present	Something that is true about the present.	Juan works in a department store.
Future	Something that will happen in the future.	He is going to / will study architecture in college.

Simple Tenses

Subject	Past	Present	Future	
I	spent	spend	will spend	more time with my brothers.
You	enjoyed	enjoy	will enjoy	being a mother.
He, She, It	studied	studies	will study	English every day.
We	put	put	will put	our studies first.
They	worked	work	will work	too many hours.

Be

Subject	Past	Present	Future
I	was	am	will be
you	were	are	will be
he, she, it	was	is	will be
we	were	are	will be
they	were	are	will be

Past Perfect

Subject	Had/Hadn't	Past participle	Complement	Clause
I, he, she, we, you, they	had / hadn't	trained	for six months	before I ran the marathon
		(already) taken	English classes	when I started college
		studied	at the university	I went to medical school*

*After I had studied at the university, I went to medical school.

• The past perfect can show an event that happened before another event in the past.
• The past perfect can show that something happened before the verb in the *when* clause.
*The past perfect can show something that happened after another event. In this case the *after* clause includes the past perfect and the clauses are separated with a comma.

Future Perfect Tense

Subject	Will Have	Past participle		Second future event (present tense)
I	will have	become	a teacher	by the time my kids are in school.
He	will have	been	a graphic designer (for five years)	when he turns 35.
They	will have	found	a job	by the time I finish school.

• We use the future perfect to talk about an activity that will be completed before another time or event in the future. **Note:** The order of events is not important. If the second future event comes first, use a comma.

By the time my kids are in school, I will have become a teacher.

Future Perfect Continuous: *Will have been* + Verb + *ing*

Example sentence	Duration	Future event or action
She **will have been studying** architecture for three years by the time she gets her degree.	three years	gets her degree
They **will have been working** at the same job for twenty years when they retire.	twenty years	retire

- Use the *future perfect continuous* to emphasize **the duration** of an activity that leads up to a future time or event.

Note: The *future perfect* is used in a similar way, but it doesn't emphasize duration.

Future Perfect Tense

Completed future event	Second future event
I **will have saved** $3,000	by the time he arrives.
You **will have paid** off the house	when you reach retirement.
They **will have found** jobs	by the time they finish school.

We use the **future perfect** to talk about an activity that will be completed before another time or event in the future.

Past Perfect Continuous Tense

First past activity					Second past event
Subject	*Had*	*Been*	*-ing* verb		Simple past
Sheila	had	been	buying	designer clothes	before she started bargain shopping.
Sam	had	been	making	coffee at home	before he began buying it at a coffee shop.
They	had	been	paying	a higher deductible	before they called the insurance company.

We use the past perfect continuous to talk about an activity that was happening for a while before another event that happened in the past. For the more recent event, we use the simple past.

Modals: *Can* and *Could* (Ability)

Subject	Modal	Base	Complement
I, you, he, she, it, we, they	can could	save invest spend	our money my savings his earnings

- Use *can* as a modal to express ability or what is possible to do. Use *could* with the same verb to express a suggestion or a possibility.

    We can invest our money in a CD. (expresses ability)

    We could invest our money in a CD. (expresses ability but only as a suggestion)

Modals: *Should* and *Ought to* (Advisability)

Subject	Modal	*have* + participle	Complement
I, you, he, she, it, we, they	should ought to	have looked	for errors
		have checked	our credit report

- Use *should* or *ought to* interchangeably. When used with *have* and the past participle, they express advice about something done in the past.

Modals: *May, Might,* and *Could* (Uncertainty)

Subject	Modal	*have* + participle	Complement
it	may	have gotten	stolen online
someone, he, she, they	might	have found	your social security number
it	could	have been	identity theft

- Use modals like *may, might,* and *could* with *have* and the past participle to describe possibility or uncertainty in something that happened in the past.

  It could have been identity theft. (The speaker doesn't know. He or she is expressing the possibility. He or she is uncertain of what really happened.)

Future Modals: *Should, Ought to, May, Might,* and *Could* (Uncertainty)

Example (modal + base verb)	Rule
He *should* report the identity theft. (He *shouldn't* report the identity theft.) He *ought to* report the identity theft. (He *ought not* report the identity theft.)	We use *should* or *ought to* to give a strong suggestion. However, we are uncertain if it will happen.
They *may/might/could* check his credit information once a month. (They *may/might/could* not check his credit information once a month.)	We use *may, might,* and *could* to show uncertainty about what will happen in the future. *May* is more certain than *might* or *could*.

Future Continuous

Example	Rule
We **will be working** on the budget **when** the financial planner arrives.	to show when an action (simple present) interrupts a continuous action in the future (future continuous)
At 8:00 A.M. we **will be working** on the budget.	to express an action at a specific time in the future—an action that started before that time
We **will be working** on the budget while **you are talking** on the phone.	to show when two continuous actions will be happening at the same time in the future
Note: The future tense cannot be used in clauses. Therefore in the first example, we use the simple present and in the third example, we use the present continuous.	

Causative Verbs: *Get, Have, Help, Make, Let*			
Subject	**Verb**	**Noun/Pronoun (object)**	**Infinitive (omit *to* except for *get*)**
He	will get	his handyman	to come.
She	had	her mom	wait for the repairperson.
The landlord	helped	me	move in.
Melanie	makes	her sister	pay half of the rent.
Mr. Martin	let	Melanie	skip one month's rent.

- Transitive verbs are verbs that require a direct object. Causative verbs are usually transitive verbs.

Perception Verbs		
Subject + verb	**Direct object**	**Gerund or Base**
Simple Present		
I see / watch / look at	the landlord	fixing the sink.
I notice / observe	the gardener	clipping bushes on Tuesday.
I feel	the light switch in the dark.	
I hear / listen to	music	filling the room.
I smell	a strange odor.	
Simple Past		
I saw / watched / looked at	my neighbor	water (watering) the plants.
I noticed / observed	everything that went on there.	
I felt	the cold water	run (running).
I heard / listened to	noises	come (coming) from upstairs.
I smelled	a sweet smell.	

- Transitive verbs require a direct object. Perception verbs are usually transitive verbs.

- In the present tense, use the gerund if needed after the direct object. **Note:** In most of the examples above, the gerund is not needed. It just adds more information.

- In the past tense, use the base or gerund after the direct object.

Comparative and Superlative Adjectives

Type of adjective	Simple form	Comparative form	Superlative form
One-syllable adjectives	high	**higher**	**the highest**
One-syllable adjectives that end in -e	nice	**nicer**	**the nicest**
One-syllable adjectives that end in *consonant-vowel-consonant*	big	**bigger**	**the biggest**
Two-syllable adjectives that end in -y	pricey	**pricier**	**the priciest**
Other two-syllable adjectives	decent	**more decent**	**the most decent**
Some two-syllable adjectives have two forms	quiet friendly	**quieter** *or* **more quiet** **friendlier** *or* **more friendly**	**the quietest** *or* **the most quiet** **the friendliest** or **the most friendly**
Adjectives with three or more syllables	expensive	**more expensive**	**the most expensive**

- Use the comparative form to compare two things.
- If the second item is expressed, use *than*.
    My apartment is **bigger than** hers.
- Use the superlative form to compare one thing to two or more things.
- A prepositional phrase is sometimes used at the end of a superlative sentence.
    My automobile mechanic is the nicest repairman **in the business**.

	Simple Form	Comparative Form	Superlative Form
Irregular Adjectives	good bad far little much/many	better worse farther less more	the best the worst the farthest the least the most
Irregular Adverbs	well badly a little a lot	better worse less more	the best the worst the least the most

Adverbial Clauses of Time		
Main clause (independent clause)	Subordinate conjunction	Subordinate clause (dependent clause)
I spoke to you	after	you examined me on Friday.
Don't pay anything	before	you get an itemized bill.
She felt sicker	when	she saw the bill.
He made the co-pay	while	she was being examined.
We'll send your bill	as soon as	your insurance pays their portion.
She explained the situation	once	the patient calmed down.

• The time clause can also go first and is followed by a comma.

After you called me on Friday, I spoke to you.

While she was being examined, he made the co-pay.

• Subordinate adverbial clauses have a subject and verb construction, but are dependent on the main clause for their meaning.

Adverbial Clauses of Reason		
Main clause	Subordinate conjunction	Subordinate clause (dependent clause)
Health insurance is important	because	you never know when there might be an emergency.
The insurance paid the bill	since	we paid all the premiums on time.
The insurance questioned the charges	as	we had quite a few visits in one month.
You can get hip surgery	now that	you have health insurance.
He will keep the PPO	as long as	the premiums don't get too expensive.

• The reason clause can also go first and is followed by a comma.

Since we paid all the premiums on time, the insurance paid.
As long as the premiums don't get too expensive, we will keep the PPO.

• Subordinate adverbial clauses have a subject and verb construction, but are dependent on the main clause for their meaning. Adverbial clauses of reason tell why something happens or is done.

Adverbial Clauses of Concession

Main clause	Subordinate conjunction	Subordinate clause (dependent clause)
He says he doesn't have a gambling problem	although	he spends a lot of time in Vegas.
She tries to stop eating so much	though	she still eats over 4000 calories a day.
He smokes 3 packs of cigarettes a day	even though	he says he is quitting.
We are good students	in spite of the fact that	we are addicted to shopping.
The doctor said to take the medicine	even if	I don't like the taste.

* *though* is the same as *although* but less formal. *Even though* shows a stronger contrast.

• The clause of concession can always go first and is offset from the main clause by a comma.

Although he spends a lot of time in Vegas, he says he doesn't have a gambling problem.
Even though he says he is quitting, he smokes 3 packs of cigarettes a day.

• Subordinate adverbial clauses have a subject and verb construction, but are dependent on the main clause for their meaning. Adverbial clauses of concession show a contrast to the main clause.

Adverbial Clauses of Condition 1

Main clause	Subordinate conjunction	Subordinate clause (dependent clause)	
The doctor will be unhappy	if	you don't take your medication.	
She will be on time for her appointment	unless	the bus is late.	has the opposite meaning of *if*
They will be on time for the appointment	provided that	the bus is on time.	has a similar meaning to *if*
He will get better	only if	he follows the doctor's instructions.	more definite than *if*

• The clause of condition can always go first and is offset from the main clause by a comma.

If you don't take your medicine, the doctor will not be happy.

• Subordinate adverbial clauses have a subject and verb construction, but are dependent on the main clause for their meaning. Adverbial clauses of condition show the circumstances when the main clause is true.

Adverbial Clauses of Condition 2

Main clause	Subordinate conjunction	Subordinate clause (dependent clause)
You should take an aspirin a day	whether or not	you have any chest pains.
You should always be prepared	in case	there is an emergency.
You should get a second opinion	even if	you are satisfied with the first.

- The clause of condition can always go first and is offset from the main clause by a comma.

Even if you are satisfied with the first opinion, you should get a second.

- Subordinate adverbial clauses have a subject and verb construction, but are dependent on the main clause for their meaning. Adverbial clauses of condition show the circumstances when the main clause is true.

Adjective Clauses That Modify Indefinite Pronouns

Person (who)	She is someone *who sells her fair share of cars*. Anybody *who shops like he does* must have a lot of money.
Thing (*that* or *which*)	Everything *(that) they bought* had to be returned. Anything *that glowed* she wanted to have.

Indefinite pronouns are pronouns that are not specific like *someone* and *anything*.
Indefinite pronouns include:

   another, anyone, anybody, anything, everyone, everybody, everything, nothing, each, either, no one, neither, nobody, one, someone, somebody, something, both, few, many, several

Adjective Clauses with Subject Pronouns

	Adjective clause	Clause construction		
		relative pronoun	+	verb
Person (*whom*)	She is the salesperson *who was in the store yesterday.* The salesperson *who was in the store yesterday* was excellent. (*Who* is the subject of the adjective clauses and modifies the preceding noun.)	who	+	was
Thing (*that* or *which*)	They bought the patio furniture *that was on sale*. The furniture *which is on sale* is beautiful. (*That* and *which* are the subject of the adjective clauses and modify the preceding noun.)	that which	+ +	was is

- Restrictive adjective clauses give essential information.

   They bought the patio furniture *that was on sale.* This means there was some furniture that wasn't on sale and the clause specifies only the furniture on sale.

- Nonrestrictive adjective clauses give extra unnecessary information. Use commas to offset the clause and use *which* not *that* for things.

   They bought the patio furniture, *which was on sale.* This means all the furniture was on sale and the information was not necessary to distinguish it from other furniture.

Adjective Clauses Using *When*, *Where*, or *Why*

	Adjective clause	Clause construction		
		relative adverb +	**subject** +	**verb**
Place	The store *where we bought the furniture* didn't offer a product guarantee.	where	we	bought
	We bought a new guitar at a store *where they don't offer service guarantees*.	where	they	don't offer
Time	We bought the computer on the day *when they were offering extended warranties*.	when	they	were offering
	She never thought she'd see the day *when you could buy things on the internet*.	when	you	could buy
Reason	The reason *why they didn't buy the printer* is it printed too slowly.	why	they	didn't buy
	Slow service is the reason *why we never shop at that store*.	why	we	never shop

All adjective clauses have three essential components: 1. They contain a subject and a verb; 2. They begin with either a relative pronoun, *who, whom, whose, that* or *which*; or a relative adverb, *where, when,* or *why*; and 3. They function as an adjective.

Adjective Clauses with *Whose*

Replacing a possessive adjective	Clause construction
I want to buy a cat. *Its* lineage should be purebred. **Converts to:** I want to buy a cat *whose* lineage is purebred.	*Whose* replaces a *possessive adjective* that precedes a person or a thing. It refers to both animate and inanimate nouns.
Robert bought a new TV. *His* old TV was broken. **Converts to:** Robert, *whose* old TV was broken, bought a new one.	
The family just moved in. *Their* house is for sale. **Converts to:** The family *whose* house is for sale just moved in.	*whose* + noun + verb

- The rule for restrictive and nonrestrictive clauses applies to these adjective clauses as well. When the clause is necessary for clarity, no commas are used to offset it.

Nouns: Phrases, Pronouns, Clauses

Definition	Example sentences
Pronouns: words that take the place of nouns including subject pronouns, object pronouns, possessive pronouns, and reflexive pronouns.	*It* is difficult. (subject) Javier loves *it*. (object) His computer is over there next to *mine*. (possessive) She sees *herself* in an office job in two years. (reflexive)
Noun phrase: a group of words with a noun as the main word.	*His job* is difficult. They need *three computers* for *the office*.
Noun clause: A group of words that have a subject and verb. The clause may function as a noun. It can be the subject or object of a sentence.	*What he does* is difficult. (subject) He loves *what he does*. (object)

Noun Clauses as Objects of Prepositions

	Preposition	Noun clause = object of the preposition
We are concerned	about	*what* she needs to do.
I am interested	in	*what* you have to say.
We can't decide	on	*who* we want for the new supervisor.
We went	to	*where* the paper was stored.
I spoke	about	*how* he treated other employees.

- A noun clause as the object of a preposition starts with a question word and is followed by a subject and verb.

Noun Clauses as Complements

Subject	Verb	Noun clause = Complement	Clause construction
It	seems	*that they work together well as a team.*	*that* + subject + verb
They	are	*what we would call well-organized.*	
She	became	*what they considered a problem in the office.*	
He	got	*what he wanted.*	*what* + subject + verb
You	felt	*what I said had merit, didn't you?*	

A complement always follows "to be", "to become", "to get", "to feel", or "to seem."

Noun Clauses as Subjects

Noun clause = Subject	Verb	
That our whole department got a raise	was	a surprise to us.
What we did yesterday	made	a big difference in office efficiency.
How she did her job	benefited	everyone.
Where I went	is	none of your business.
How they spoke to us	helped	me understand my job.

- A noun clause as a subject of the verb starts with a question word or *that* and is followed by a subject and verb.

Noun Clauses as Objects of Verbs

Subject + Verb	Noun clause	Explanation
I did	*what* I was asked.	• A noun clause as an object of the verb starts with a question word or *that* and is followed by a subject and verb.
She knows	*how* to do a PowerPoint presentation.	
They decided	*where* the location would be.	• In this case, the noun clauses are the object of the sentence.
My boss asked	*who* would be best for the job.	
I hope	*that* they worked as a team.	

Noun Clauses with *Whether* and *If*

Expression	*whether/if*	Clause
I don't know	*if*	we will keep our jobs (or not).
I wanted to know	*whether*	(or not) we would work Monday.
We discussed	*if*	he would continue with the project (or not).

- Use *whether* or *if* for statements where there is doubt to something being true or false. Using *or not* is optional but falls in a different place depending on which word you use. Either word can be used.

- *Whether* and *if* statements are sometimes considered embedded questions. Consider the following:

Will we keep our jobs?	I don't know if we will keep our jobs.
Would we work tomorrow?	I wanted to know whether we will work Monday.
Would he continue?	We discussed if he would continue.

Articles: *A*, *An*, and *The*

Rules (article + noun)	Example	What it means
a* or *an Use *a* or *an* when the noun that follows represents one of a class of things or when the sentence is making a generalization. *An* is used when the noun that follows starts with a vowel sound.	***A* citizen** has specific rights.	a citizen = any citizen or just citizens in general; sometimes the speaker means all citizens
the Use *the* when the listener and the speaker both have the same specific idea in mind represented by the noun.	***The* citizen** we spoke about yesterday has his rights.	the citizen = a specific person who has already been identified

Note: Singular count nouns must be preceded by an article, *this/that,* or a possessive adjective.

Definite Articles vs. Nothing

Rules (article + noun)	Example	What it means
the Use *the* when the listener and the speaker both have the same specific idea in mind represented by the noun.	*The* rights that citizens have include the right to vote.	the rights = specific rights outlined in the U.S. Constitution
Ø Use no article with plural nouns when making generalizations.	*Citizens* have specific rights.	citizens = any citizen or just citizens in general; sometimes the speaker means all citizens
Ø Use no article with noncount nouns when making generalizations.	*Justice* is another word for *fairness* under the law.	justice and fairness = generalizations that cannot be counted
Ø Use no article with proper names unless the article is part of the name (The United States of America.)	*Judge Harvey Spanner* declared his support for the new mayor.	Judge Harvey Spanner = the name of the judge

Note: Singular count nouns must be preceded by an article, *this/that*, or a possessive adjective.

Demonstrative Determiners and Pronouns

	Singular	Plural
Near	*this*	*these*
Far	*that*	*those*

Demonstratives determiners (or *adjectives*) tell the reader if the noun is near or far and singular or plural. *Demonstrative pronouns* represent a noun that is near or far and singular or plural. Nouns can be omitted if referred to previously.

	Examples	
Near (space)	*This* (trash can) is used for recycling.	The trash can is near the speaker.
Far (space)	*That* (trash can) is used for recycling.	The trash can is not within reaching distance of the speaker.
Near (time)	*These* (recycling systems) we learned about are great.	They learned about the recycling system a short time ago, probably the same day.
Far (time)	*Those* (recycling systems) we learned about are great.	They learned about the recycling system previously.

Such and Demonstrative Determiners

Determiner	Example	Explanation
this + noun Use *this* with singular nouns that represent specific things.	Her opinion is that we should all carpool. Is *this* opinion really based on reality?	*This* refers to the specific opinion that everyone should carpool.
such a(n) + noun Use *such a* with singular nouns that represent classes or subgroups of the nouns.	Her opinion is that we should all carpool. Is *such an* opinion really based on reality?	*Such an* is referring to any opinion like the one mentioned and not only the opinion that everyone should carpool.
these + noun Use *these* with plural nouns that represent specific things.	Carpool lanes with walls on either side can be dangerous in accidents. *These* lanes are difficult to merge in and out of.	*These* lanes refers only to the specific carpool lanes with walls on either side.
such + noun Use *such* with plural nouns that represent classes or groups that have been specified.	Carpool lanes with walls on either side can be dangerous in accidents. *Such* lanes are also difficult to merge in and out of.	*Such* lanes refers to all of those carpool lanes with walls on either side.

Use *this* or *such* with noncount nouns. Use *this* for specific and *such* for general.

Contrary-to-Fact Conditionals: Statements

Condition (*if* + subject + past tense verb)	Result (subject + *would* + base verb)
If I **had** a million dollars,	I **would buy** a new house.
If you **didn't have** so much work,	you **would take** a long vacation.
If she **were** a smart consumer,	she **would read** sales ads carefully.
If I **weren't** busy,	I **would shop** around.

- A contrary-to-fact statement is a sentence that is not true at this point in time.
- A comma is used between the two clauses when the *if*-clause comes first.
- The *if*-clause can come first or second. When it comes second, no comma is used.
    I would buy a new house **if I had** a million dollars.
- In the *if*-clause, use *were* instead of *was* with *I, he, she,* and *it*.

Contrary-to-fact Conditionals: *Yes/No* Questions

if + subject + past tense / *would* + subject + base verb	Short answer	
If you **had** more money, **would you buy** a car?	Yes, I **would**.	No, I **wouldn't**.
If he **didn't have** so much work, **would he take** a vacation?	Yes, he **would**.	No, he **wouldn't**.
If they **weren't** busy, **would they shop** around?	Yes, they **would**.	No, they **wouldn't**.

- A *yes/no* question in a contrary-to-fact conditional is formed in the result clause.
- The *if*-clause can come first or second. When it comes second, no comma is used.
    Would you buy a car **if you had** more money?

➤ IRREGULAR VERB FORMS

Base form	Simple past	Past participle	Base form	Simple past	Past participle
be	was, were	been	lose	lost	lost
become	became	became	make	made	made
begin	began	begun	mean	meant	meant
break	broke	broken	meet	met	met
bring	brought	brought	pay	paid	paid
build	built	built	put	put	put
buy	bought	bought	read	read	read
catch	caught	caught	ride	rode	ridden
come	came	come	run	ran	run
cost	cost	cost	say	said	said
do	did	done	sell	sold	sold
drink	drank	drunk	send	sent	sent
drive	drove	driven	set	set	set
eat	ate	eaten	show	showed	shown
fall	fell	fallen	sit	sat	sat
feel	felt	felt	sleep	slept	slept
fight	fought	fought	speak	spoke	spoken
find	found	found	spend	spent	spent
fly	flew	flown	spread	spread	spread
get	got	gotten	stand	stood	stood
give	gave	given	steal	stole	stolen
go	went	gone	take	took	taken
grow	grew	grown	teach	taught	taught
have	had	had	tell	told	told
hold	held	held	think	thought	thought
hurt	hurt	hurt	throw	threw	thrown
keep	kept	kept	wake	woke	woken
know	knew	known	wear	wore	worn
learn	learned	learned/learnt	win	won	won
lend	lent	lent	write	wrote	written

Regular verbs

Base: work   **Infinitive:** to work

Simple present	Present continuous	Simple past	Future
I work	I am working	I worked	I will work
You work	You are working	You worked	You will work
We work	We are working	We worked	We will work
They work	They are working	They worked	They will work
He works	He is working	He worked	He will work
She works	She is working	She worked	She will work
It works	It is working	It worked	It will work

Past perfect	Past continuous	Present perfect continuous	Past perfect
I have worked	I was working	I have been working	I had worked
You have worked	You were working	You have been working	You had worked
We have worked	We were working	We have been working	We had worked
They have worked	They were working	They have been working	They had worked
He has worked	He was working	He has been working	He had worked
She has worked	She was working	She has been working	She had worked
It has worked	It was working	It has been working	It had worked

---

Base: study   **Infinitive:** to study

Simple present	Present continuous	Simple past	Future
I study	I am studying	I studied	I will study
You study	You are studying	You studied	You will study
We study	We are studying	We studied	We will study
They study	They are studying	They studied	They will study
He studies	He is studying	He studied	He will study
She studies	She is studying	She studied	She will study
It studies	It is studying	It studied	It will study

Past perfect	Past continuous	Present perfect continuous	Past perfect
I have studied	I was studying	I have been studying	I had studied
You have studied	You were studying	You have been studying	You had studied
We have studied	We were studying	We have been studying	We had studied
They have studied	They were studying	They have been studying	They had studied
He has studied	He was studying	He has been studying	He had studied
She has studied	She was studying	She has been studying	She had studied
It has studied	It was studying	It has been studying	It had studied

Irregular verbs

Base: have   Infinitive: to have

Simple present	Present continuous	Simple past	Future
I have	I am having	I had	I will have
You have	You are having	You had	You will have
We have	We are having	We had	We will have
They have	They are having	They had	They will have
He has	He is having	He had	He will have
She has	She is having	She had	She will have
It has	It is having	It had	It will have

Past perfect	Past continuous	Present perfect continuous	Past perfect
I have had	I was having	I have been having	I had had
You have had	You were having	You have been having	You had had
We have had	We were having	We have been having	We had had
They have had	They were having	They have been having	They had had
He has had	He was having	He has been having	He had had
She has had	She was having	She has been having	She had had
It has had	It was having	It has been having	It had had

Base: run   Infinitive: to run

Simple present	Present continuous	Simple past	Future
I run	I am running	I ran	I will run
You run	You are running	You ran	You will run
We run	We are running	We ran	We will run
They run	They are running	They ran	They will run
He runs	He is running	He ran	He will run
She runs	She is running	She ran	She will run
It runs	It is running	It ran	It will run

Past perfect	Past continuous	Present perfect continuous	Past perfect
I have run	I was running	I have been running	I had run
You have run	You were running	You have been running	You had run
We have run	We were running	We have been running	We had run
They have run	They were running	They have been running	They had run
He has run	He was running	He has been running	He had run
She has run	She was running	She has been running	She had run
It has run	It was running	It has been running	It had run

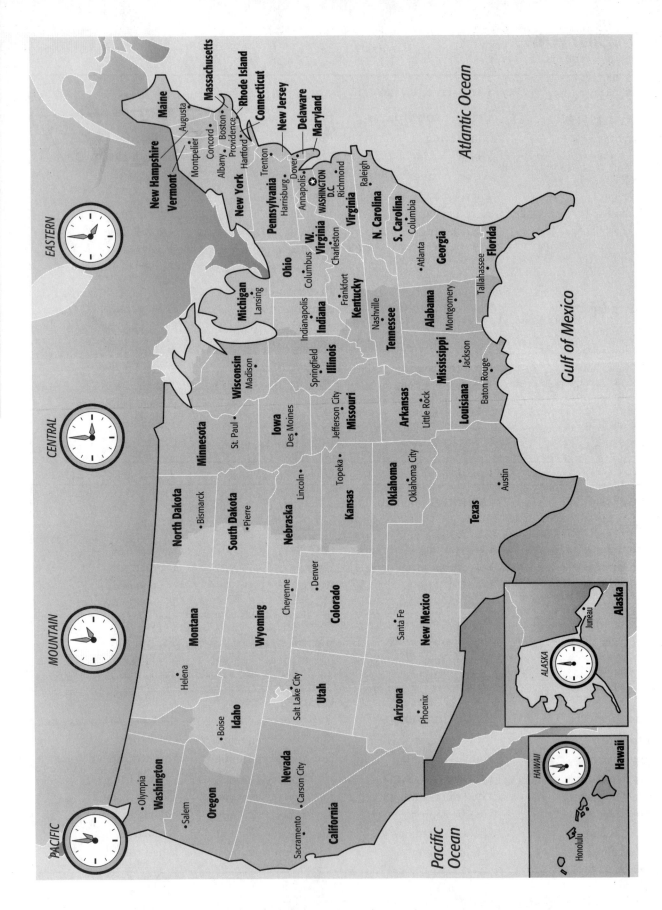

Map of the United States

Atlantic Ocean

Gulf of Mexico

Pacific Ocean

EASTERN

CENTRAL

MOUNTAIN

PACIFIC

ALASKA

HAWAII

Maine · Augusta
New Hampshire · Montpelier
Vermont · Concord
Massachusetts · Boston
Rhode Island · Providence
Connecticut · Hartford
New York · Albany
New Jersey · Trenton
Pennsylvania · Harrisburg
Delaware · Dover
Maryland · Annapolis
WASHINGTON D.C.
W. Virginia · Charleston
Virginia · Richmond
Ohio · Columbus
N. Carolina · Raleigh
S. Carolina · Columbia
Kentucky · Frankfort
Michigan · Lansing
Indiana · Indianapolis
Tennessee · Nashville
Georgia · Atlanta
Alabama · Montgomery
Florida · Tallahassee
Wisconsin · Madison
Illinois · Springfield
Missouri · Jefferson City
Mississippi · Jackson
Louisiana · Baton Rouge
Arkansas · Little Rock
Minnesota · St. Paul
Iowa · Des Moines
Nebraska · Lincoln
Kansas · Topeka
Oklahoma · Oklahoma City
North Dakota · Bismarck
South Dakota · Pierre
Texas · Austin
Montana · Helena
Wyoming · Cheyenne
Colorado · Denver
New Mexico · Santa Fe
Arizona · Phoenix
Idaho · Boise
Utah · Salt Lake City
Washington · Olympia
Oregon · Salem
Nevada · Carson City
California · Sacramento
Alaska · Juneau
Hawaii · Honolulu